Literature in Perspective

Of recent years, the ordinary man who reads for pleasure has been gradually excluded from that great debate in which every intelligent reader of the classics takes part. There are two reasons for this: first, so much criticism floods from the world's presses that no one but a scholar living entirely among books can hope to read it all; and second, the critics and analysts, mostly academics, use a language that only their fellows in the same discipline can understand.

Consequently criticism, which should be as 'inevitable as breathing'—an activity for which we are all qualified—has become the private field of a few warring factions who shout their unintelligible battle cries to each other but make little communication to the common man.

Literature in Perspective aims at giving a straightforward account of literature and of writers—straightforward both in content and in language. Critical jargon is as far as possible avoided; any terms that must be used are explained simply; and the constant preoccupation of the authors of the Series is to be lucid.

It is our hope that each book will be easily understood, that it will adequately describe its subject without pretentiousness so that the intelligent reader who wants to know about Dryden or Keats or Shakespeare will find enough in it to bring him up to date on critical estimates.

Even those who are well read, we believe, can benefit from a lucid exposition of what they may have taken for granted, and perhaps—dare it be said?—not fully understood.

K. H. G.

Dryden

This is a study of John Dryden's poetry by one who finds his alert mind stimulating, his technical skill fascinating, and his attitudes often infuriating.

Because his work stems directly from his cultural environment, Dryden is at the mercy of historical critics who quote his poems merely to illustrate the state of 17th-century politics. Because Dryden was interested in ideas, other critics bury his verse deep among their erudite footnotes. Though I am willing to be led by any scholar towards what Dryden called the *explication* of a poem, it is the taste of his words on my own tongue which really satisfies me.

This study, therefore, after highlighting significant features of the background, turns its attention to the foreground—the poems themselves—and offers a methodical, detailed and yet personal commentary upon the remarkable range of songs, elegies, descriptions, satires, polemics and persuasions. I admire a man who can write both saucy songs and Roman Catholic elegies, devising the appropriate form for each, and to follow sympathetically Dryden's experiments with words and topics is to extend the range of our own sensitivity. The Restoration period was an immense charade masking the birthpangs of modern England, and Dryden's rococo finery has a steel framework of earnest concern for man and society.

Quotations are from James Kinsley's *The Poems of John Dryden*, Clarendon Press, Oxford, 4 vols., 1958, but the spelling has been modernised.

I would like to thank Patrick McCaughey for help in choosing the illustrations; Harold Love for the temporary loan of books and the permanent loan of ideas; Norma Bolton for technical assistance with the typescript. My long-distance debts are in particular to lectures on the 17th century by Geoffrey Bullough and L. C. Knights, to the writings of Christopher Hill and V. de Sola Pinto, and to the verse-speaking of Francis Berry.

D. D.

Literature in Perspective

Dryden

Dennis Davison

Evans Brothers Limited, London

Published by Evans Brothers Limited
Montague House, Russell Square, London, W.C.1
© Dennis Davison 1968
First published 1968

00025626

Set in 11 on 12 point Bembo and printed in Great Britain
by The Camelot Press Ltd., London and Southampton

237   44367   8 cased   PR 4456
237   44380   5 limp

Contents

THE PERSPECTIVE   *page* 9

1. Politics and Religion   13

2. Education and Neo-Classicism   20

3. Science Demands the Muse   29

4. Verse Technique: the Heroic Couplet   39

THE POEMS

5. Songs and Music Odes   57

6. Elegies   73

7. Verse Journalism: *Annus Mirabilis*   92

8. Satires   106

9. Poems of Persuasion   133

Bibliography   147

Index   150

The Author

Dennis Davison, Litt.B., M.A., Ph.D., is Senior Lecturer in English at Monash University, Melbourne, Australia.

Acknowledgements

The author and publishers are indebted to the Curators of the Bodleian Library, Oxford, for permission to reproduce the cover portrait; to the Marchioness of Cholmondeley for the painting of the Presentation of a Pineapple to Charles II and to the Royal Society for the painting of Brouncker, Charles II and Bacon. The painting of the Sea Triumph of Charles II is reproduced by gracious permission of Her Majesty the Queen.

They are also indebted to Thomas Nelson & Sons Ltd. for permission to reprint an extract from *The Century of Revolution* by Christopher Hill; to the University of North Carolina Press for an extract from *The Life of John Dryden* by Charles E. Ward, and to the University of Chicago Press for permission to reprint from *Satires and Epistles of Horace* by Smith Palmer Bovie, © 1959 by the University of Chicago.

The Perspective

Rather more than a century before Dryden's time artists such as Botticelli, Leonardo da Vinci and Dürer developed the art of perspective as part of the general trend towards a more naturalistic depiction of the visible world. Instead of the quaint, flat, disproportioned medieval paintings the new ones gave the illusion of reality as it appeared to the eye of the beholder, in which everything seemed to be its correct size and was properly related, in space, to other objects and to the background. Today we use the phrase: 'to see something in its proper perspective', meaning that we judge the value of an object, or a person, in relation to its environment and its place in time. And one way of looking at works of literature is to study them in the context of their period, of the contemporary 'climate of ideas' (to use a 17th-century phrase), and against the history of previous literature.

We are not obliged to study literature in this way. No law has yet been passed to this effect. Literary criticism, unlike the Christian religion, is not established by law—though Bishop Samuel Parker, in Dryden's lifetime, did propose that metaphors should be abolished from sermons by Act of Parliament, and Dryden himself, the Father of Literary Criticism and a strong supporter of an English Academy, often used a dictatorial tone when describing the proper method of writing literature: 'The poet is bound, and that *ex officio*, to give his reader some one precept of moral virtue, and to caution him against some one particular vice or folly.'

Indeed one feature of our century is the rise of a school of Anti-Historical Critics who expressly claim that literature must be examined *out of perspective*, and in isolation from the context in which it grew. The pure value of a poem, for instance, lies in its timeless quality, its impact upon the modern reader *now*, and speculation about why it was written, what people several centuries ago felt when they read it, or the relation of this particular poem to similar poems written before it, is, say these critics, irrelevant and dangerous. If we can enjoy a piece of cake without studying the history of agriculture or the chemistry of cooking, why cannot we enjoy a poem without tracing its genesis in the intellectual background of the period or the poet's unconscious? When we sit on a chair we demand that it should look beautiful and feel comfortable. We do not want to know how it was made, the cost of French polish, or whether the man who made it was suffering from a mother-fixation. And these critics ask, formidably, how can you place an author against the history of his times, when twenty different historians will give you twenty different accounts of the period?

On Mondays, Wednesdays and Fridays I agree with these critics, asserting, with Gertrude Stein, that 'a rose is a rose is a rose'—in other words, that a poem, like a rose, is an end-product. How the rose was produced, the earth it was planted in, the manure that stimulated it, and so on, are of great interest to the gardener or the biologist, but such information is not relevant to our appreciation of its beauty. Background knowledge, partial and second-hand as it must be, distracts us from the personal, direct appreciation of the rose, or the poem. We are concerned with what is alive in the poem *for us, today*, not with what might have been alive for other readers in the past. In this way a poem is a special and different experience for each reader—even different each time he reads it. Each person's reaction to a poem is subjective, a private relationship established between himself and the poem. No third person has the right to intervene, to alter that relationship, much less to test the reader's response by an examination and impertinently assess that response with a mark.

However, on Tuesdays, Thursdays and Saturdays I feel more sympathetic to the Contextual Critics. After all, I reflect, poems, unlike roses and chairs, are made of words, and have a meaningful content which connects them with the words of other men and other times. Also, although a poem is an end-product, and appears to be a separate object isolated from its environment, it does make reference to that environment and it does invite us, as well, to proceed again from the world of the poem to the larger world which gave it birth. A poem is not a pure, subjective experience, but something which comes trailing clouds of associations which it has absorbed from other poems, from other people, from society, from tradition. It is impossible to read Milton's *Paradise Lost* and pretend that it does not remind us of the *Book of Genesis*. And how can we appreciate Shakespeare if we do not understand the Elizabethan World Picture, or Chaucer's *Tales* unless we ask scholars the meaning of his obsolete vocabulary? Reading a poem is a complex, co-operative venture, full of uncertainties, but richly rewarding because it forces us to relate the work of art to the fascinating human context of which it is part. Poetry is about life, and it is written by a particular person in a particular period, using ideas and words and verse-forms related intimately to himself and his times. The more we know about the background to a poem, the more we shall see the foreground, the poem itself, in true perspective.

And then of course comes Sunday, when my scepticism about these conflicting views results in the sort of bewilderment which Dryden seems to have felt in *Religio Laici*, confronted as he was with age-old theological disputes and the rival claims of philosophers and churches to be the 'unerring guide' to truth. And it is because Dryden's century was the battleground for fierce religious and social controversy, which still blinds us with its dust and provokes us to take sides, that it is specially valid to raise this critical problem of whether we should attempt to read his poems in perspective (if we can discover it) or out of perspective (if we can ignore it). Indeed one of the main themes running through recent Dryden studies is that of trying to assess what is lastingly valuable in a body of poetry which sprang so directly out of the events of the times. I think few poets have provoked more varying critical estimates than has Dryden, who in his own day was often the centre of dispute. And so, as literary criticism is still a free and voluntary activity (despite some recent attempts to make it an exact science whose pronouncements are binding on all), I would suggest that all types of approaches—anti-historical, contextual, biographical, psychological, formal, Marxist, existentialist, statistical, etc., should be encouraged in that spirit of toleration that the 17th century eventually learned to value. After all, to borrow yet another significant notion from this century, these varying approaches can be tested, not merely argued about, by *experiment*. There is nothing to prevent our first reading Dryden's poems isolated from their context, and then once more in the light of any background information we wish to gather. We should then be able, by this experimental method, to discover which approach affords us the richest appreciation of them. This present study, therefore, is offered as part of the proposed literary experiment, and as I present John Dryden *in perspective* I shall be asking my readers, and myself, whether in fact our understanding and enjoyment of his verse is being increased. No critic is the 'unerring guide' that Dryden sought in the field of faith, and though for the sake of brevity I may sometimes seem to be speaking dogmatically, my intention is always to uphold the spirit of free enquiry.

I

Politics and Religion

John Dryden was born in 1631, and died in 1700, so his adult years were mainly passed in an England, comparatively at peace, under the restored monarchy and church. But the violent upheaval of the civil wars (between 1641 and 1648) and the political and religious strife of the earlier part of the century seem to have had a powerful, lifelong influence on his attitudes. In 1649, when Charles I was beheaded at the Banquet Hall, Dryden was eighteen and in his final form at Westminster School, a short walk away. He was later to write of his contemporaries (substituting Israel for England):

> The sober part of Israel, free from stain,
> Well knew the value of a peaceful reign;
> And, looking backward with a wise afright,
> Saw seams of wounds, dishonest to the sight:
> In contemplation of whose ugly scars,
> They cursed the memory of civil wars.

Here, with history and biography, begin our difficulties in putting John Dryden in perspective. The above lines, from *Absalom and Achitophel*, were written by Charles II's fifty-year-old Poet Laureate in an attack upon those who were perhaps instigating another civil war. And yet Dryden himself had lived through the Cromwellian régime, had written an elegy in praise of the Protector, and had taken a minor post in the Cromwellian bureaucracy, working alongside two celebrated poets and supporters of the usurper, John Milton and Andrew Marvell. And so the traditional picture emerges of John Dryden, the notorious turncoat, who could celebrate Cromwell in *Heroic*

13

Stanzas in 1658, and welcome Charles II with *A Poem on the Happy Restoration and Return of His Sacred Majesty . . .* in 1660. But worse is yet to come. When the Catholic Duke of York ascended the throne in 1685 his Poet Laureate, who in 1682 had written an eloquent poem in defence of the Church of England, was received into the Catholic Church. So it has not been difficult to label him as an opportunist, as a poetic Vicar of Bray. (The historian Christopher Hill, writing in 1961, can still speak of later men of letters who 'did not need to turn their coats as often or as humiliatingly as Dryden had done'.) Nevertheless the most striking thing about recent Dryden biographical studies is the contrary insistence that he was a man of integrity and firm convictions, responding with admirable consistency to the thorny problems of religion and politics.

But we shall leave this matter aside for the moment, and look briefly at the discussions, religious, political and social, which divided Englishmen for many more years than the actual military conflict. By 1641 the uneasy peace of Charles I's reign had exploded in a nation-wide armed clash between King and Parliament, and their supporters, ending in the execution of Charles in 1649, the declaration of a republic, and from 1653 to 1659 the protectorates of Oliver Cromwell, and his son Richard. In 1660 Charles II was restored to the throne. In the past, historians have seen this turbulent period as a political struggle between King and Parliament for control of the State, and as a religious conflict between Anglicanism and Puritanism (whose representatives beheaded the Archbishop of Canterbury and abolished the national church). Recent historians have shown that the social upheaval was even more fundamental than this, and that major changes were also happening in the fields of economics, science, educational theory, and literature. This general ferment of ideas, which is only now being studied in detail, and the actual changes in the political and economic structure of society, constitute for some modern historians a period of revolution, and thus the English Revolution has been called the earliest of the European bourgeois revolutions, in which power was transferred to the middle classes, finally enabling them to operate a free-market economy and rule through democratic parliaments. The English middle-class revolution had a special Puritan form and when the monarchy and the Church were restored it looked as though it had failed. The earthly paradise the Puritans had hoped to establish was lost, as many besides Milton must have felt when he wrote *Paradise Lost* in the reign of the libertine monarch. Certainly the Restoration attempted to put back the clock, but under the surface fundamental changes were continuing. One historian has exclaimed ironically that it was called the Restoration because so little was restored. As we now know, the power of the king was eventually transferred to Parliament, which dismissed James II and invited William of Orange from Holland to rule as a constitutional monarch. The Church of England tried to impose its authority over all, but eventually toleration won the day, and in the course of the next century the 'wild fanatics' such as the Quakers, the Shakers, the Congregationalists, the Baptists and the (later) fearsome Methodists became utterly respectable.

So if we compare the England of 1603 with the Great Britain of 1714 we find that by the time of Queen Anne (1702–14) Britain had a large empire in America, Asia and Africa, and the East India Company was the most powerful corporation in the country. Kings could no longer interfere in the economic life, now consisting of a free-market system regulated by parliamentary policy, the Bank of England and the National Debt (that necessary modern institution). In 1603 heretics were still burnt at the stake. By 1714 Protestant dissent was legally tolerated. Newtonian science emerged triumphant, and Reason rather than Authority was appealed to in questions of religion and politics. Astrology was replaced by astronomy, alchemy by chemistry. The belief in witchcraft, upheld stubbornly by Cambridge intellectuals and Christian ministers, one must sadly note, lost its terror among the repartee of cynical town-wits and the calm conversation of sensible gentlemen of the later 17th century. These are a few of the major changes which stemmed from the English Revolution, some of which took over a century to manifest themselves openly. And of course there are a myriad other developments in the sphere of everyday life which, if you reflect, are not unconnected with the fundamental movements of history. Christopher Hill, in *The Century of Revolution*, has itemised some of them: 'Englishmen's diet was transformed in this century by the introduction of root crops, which made it possible to have fresh meat in winter. Potatoes and many new vegetables were added to it, as were tea, coffee, chocolate, sugar and tobacco. Port- and gin-drinking became national habits. Plague was frequent in the first half of the century, extinct by the end. The modern arrangement of meals—breakfast, lunch, and dinner—dates from the 17th century. So does the modern pattern of male costume—coat, waistcoat, breeches. Calico, linen and silk came in for clothes; leather went out. By the end of the century pottery and glass had replaced pewter and wood at table; many families used knives, forks, mirrors and pocket handkerchiefs; at Chatsworth the Duke of Devonshire had installed a bath with hot and cold running water.' When we read the poets who followed Dryden, such as Pope, Gay, Prior and Swift, we are possibly amazed to discover how obsessed they are with clothes, coaches, wigs, fans, coffee-cups, tobacco-pipes, lavish meals, vegetarian diet, cutlery, silverware, ornaments, women's cosmetics, room decorations, and (especially Swift) close-stools and jakes. A lot of 17th-century urban verse is cluttered with these sometimes necessary, sometimes prestige, objects. Dryden's verse hardly ever bothers itself with such things, being much more concerned with ideas, people or national events.

Many of the more advanced ideas of the mid-century fell on stony ground: some only bore fruit centuries later. The middle-class revolution naturally was supported mainly by the urban, commercial section, often Puritan in religion, but, as V. da Sola Pinto reminds us, 'it is highly significant that a majority of the great landowning families who had made their fortunes under the Tudors . . . were either neutral or hostile to the Crown'. In addition some of the lower classes allied themselves with the gentlemen who were conducting the revolution, and proposed reforms which were too democratic to be acceptable to the middle classes. The Diggers and the Levellers, brutally suppressed by Cromwell, were really early Socialists, demanding voting rights, abolition of the House of Lords and tithes, reform of the law, and so on. Political radicalism was, after the fashion of the day, confusedly mixed with religious anarchism. A thousand sects appeared, some wildly fanatical. Quakers trembled at street corners, possessed by the divine spirit, while Ranters burnt bibles and Adamites appeared in Eden-like nudity. James Naylor entered Bristol on an ass and was welcomed as the reborn Messiah. These antics were not to the taste of 17th-century gentlemen any more than the tambourine-tapping Salvation Army lassies, singing hymns to musical-hall melodies outside rowdy public houses, were welcome to respectable 19th-century citizens (who sometimes brutally assaulted them).

Dryden always referred to these Protestant sects with amusement or contempt. In *Absalom and Achitophel* he says:

A numerous host of dreaming saints succeed;
Of the true old enthusiastic breed . . .

(His terms are loaded with irony. The Puritans had thought of themselves as 'saints' and their ecstasies and reforming zeal are dubbed 'dreaming' and 'enthusiastic'.) And politically of course the Puritans are suspected of republicanism, and they would reduce the 'kingly power' to the 'dregs of a democracy'. This derisive attitude to the 'canting crew' is only to be expected in John Dryden, Tory partisan, Anglican gentleman, and successful playwright who hobnobs with aristocratic Restoration rakes. And our modern psychologists might add that it is not unusual for men to turn ferociously against their former allegiances— for Dryden himself had come from a provincial Puritan family. But it is only fair to say that even a Puritan poet like Andrew Marvell, who wrote satires and pamphlets against Charles II and his governments, had not been able to stomach the wilder fanatics either. Praising Cromwell in *The First Anniversary* (published 1655) he denounced them more angrily, I think, than Dryden ever did:

> Accursed locusts, whom your king does spit
> Out of the centre of th'unbottomed pit;
> Wanderers, adulterers, liars, Munster's rest,
> Sorcerers, atheists, Jesuits, possessed;
> You who the scriptures and the laws deface
> With the same liberty as points and lace;
> Oh race most hypocritically strict!
> Bent to reduce us to the ancient Pict;
> Well may you act the Adam and the Eve;
> Ay, and the serpent too that did deceive.

Marvell seems particularly shocked by the naked Adamites, and others who were preaching free love. Cromwell was more conscious of the political danger of lower-class Puritanism when he said: 'I was by birth a gentleman . . . you must cut these people in pieces or they will cut you in pieces.' So the typical Restoration aversion to the Puritan sects could be found among the more respectable Cromwellian supporters, and of course in literature it had long been voiced by poets and dramatists—one remembers in particular Shakespeare's portrait of Malvolio and Ben Jonson's canting saints, Tribulation Wholesome in *The Alchemist*, or Zeal-of-the-Land Busy, who attacks the ginger-bread stall at Bartholomew Fair because it reminds him of Catholic relics, in this delightful parody of a droning Puritan: 'Hinder me not, woman. I was moved in spirit, to be here this day, in this Fair, this wicked and foul Fair; and fitter may it be called a Foul than a Fair; to protest against the abuses of it, the foul abuses of it, in regard of the afflicted saints, that are troubled, very much troubled, exceedingly troubled, with the opening of the merchandise of Babylon again, and the peeping of popery upon the stalls here, here, in the high places. See you not Goldy-locks, the purple strumpet there, in her yellow gown and green sleeves? the profane pipes, the tinkling timbrels? a shop of relics!' One has to turn to Dryden's fellow-satirist, to Butler's *Hudibras*, to recapture this comic anti-Puritan spirit. When Dryden came to write *The Hind and the Panther*, a defence of Catholicism, his hatred of Protestant sects was so great that it excluded humour almost entirely. Dryden was here out of tune with a century which was discovering the possibility of religious toleration. It is rather ironical that Dryden ended his life as a member of the persecuted Catholic minority.

2

Education and Neo-Classicism

Another aspect of the intellectual ferment in this revolutionary period was the intense interest in education—both theory and practice. Dryden's education at Westminster School, under the celebrated (or notorious) disciplinarian Dr. Busby, from about 1646 to 1650, gives us a vivid picture of the traditional classical schooling which the reformers tried, largely in vain, to abolish or modify. Charles E. Ward gives us this account: 'The day began at a quarter past five and ended twelve or fifteen hours later. After Latin prayers, morning ablutions from the common washbasin, and breakfast, the boys were marched, two by two, to their lessons. At six they began a two-hour session of repeating their grammar—Latin out of Lilly and Greek out of Camden. . . . In a semicircle before the master, they recited the rules and then made extempore verses in Latin and Greek upon themes suggested by the master. On alternate mornings, instead of making verses, they were called upon to expound some part of a Latin or Greek author, such as Cicero, Livy, Isocrates, Homer, or Xenophon. From eight to nine they were allowed time for 'beaver', a refreshment period. At nine they met for another two-hour period devoted to the reading of those exercises, in prose and in verse, which they had prepared in their rooms the night before. After lunch they came back at one o'clock for another two-hour session. On this occasion the master expounded a selection from Virgil, Cicero, Euripides or Sallust, commenting on rhetorical figures, grammatical constructions, and explaining prosody. Then followed an afternoon respite. The final meeting of the day was devoted to the repetition of a 'leaf or two' out of a book of rhetorical figures or proverbs, or sentences chosen by the master. Then a theme was assigned, upon which the student was to compose prose or verse essays in Latin or Greek before the next morning.' Some fifty years later, when he was publishing his Juvenal and Persius translations, Dryden recalled that he had translated the Third Satire of Persius 'at Westminster School, for a Thursday-night's exercise; and believe that it, and many other of my exercises of this nature in English verse, are still in the hands of my learned master, the Reverend Doctor Busby'. So it is not surprising that, when still a schoolboy, he published his first poem, *Upon the Death of the Lord Hastings*. Ironically enough Dryden's schoolmate, John Locke, the celebrated philosopher, was to write in his treatise, *Some Thoughts Concerning Education*, 1693, that if a child has poetic talent 'the parents should labour to have it stifled, and suppresssed, as much as may be: and I know not what reason a father can have, to wish his son a poet, who does not desire to have him bid defiance to all other callings and business'. Dryden, of course, our first really professional poet, did make poetry his calling and his business, though he never, unlike Alexander Pope, became very rich by it.

Restoration England was organising itself on modern lines, with its National Bank, Stock Exchange, insurance companies, national taxation, mechanised industries (primitive of course), and overseas investments, and it needed men trained in geography, mineralogy, statistics, economics, hydraulics and chemistry. What its educational system of grammar schools and two universities provided were men like John Dryden, expert in Greek and Latin language and literature. Samuel Pepys, diarist and Commissioner for the Navy, who was at Cambridge with Dryden, had to learn the multiplication table from the mate of the *Royal Charles*. John Wallis, Oxford Professor of Geometry and a member of the Royal Society, had by the age of sixteen read the Bible in Hebrew, but only became acquainted with arithmetic by accident during the Christmas holidays. Educational reformers, such as John Milton, Hartlib, Dury and Petty, wanted a wholesale reorganisation of the methods and content of education, and hundreds of schoolmasters, philosophers, writers and scientists in different ways voiced their dissatisfaction—though others opposed new-fangled ideas, as Swift was to do even in the 18th century. Milton described scathingly his years at Cambridge University, listening to 'nothing else but the scragged and thorny lectures of monkish and miserable sophistry'. John Hall, also at Cambridge, wrote sharply: 'We have hardly professors for the principal faculties, and these but lazily read—and carelessly followed.' Winstanley's comment on universities was even more pungent: 'standing ponds of stinking waters!'

The Commonwealth reformers suggested revolutionary schemes, some of which are being implemented only in our century. Briefly, they wished to reduce the study of Latin and Greek (and 'old-fashioned' logic in universities) and introduce mathematics, science, geography, modern languages and English. (University instruction was given in Latin and students were supposed to converse only in Latin, Greek or Hebrew.) Some reformers, for example, William Petty, wanted to introduce handicrafts and practical work such as making of watches and scientific instruments, gardening, confectionery, perfuming, dyeing, and 'making skeletons, and excarnating bowels'. In other words, he realised that trade schools and technical colleges were necessary for a developing commercial and industrial society. Some reformers even demanded free and compulsory education for all classes. Abraham Cowley, whose ingenious poetry was so admired by Dryden, offered detailed plans for a scientific college, and attached school, freely open to talent. Every scientific and practical subject was to be studied with urgent intensity—in fact Cowley's zeal rather comically reveals itself in his plan for an officer to stop idle talk at mealtimes and ensure that the professors only chat about their subjects.

One of the most damning things about Restoration society is that it almost entirely neglected to modernise its education, to the exasperation of Samuel Pepys and others, who realised how essential it was for a commercial, scientific age to train businessmen, civil servants, politicians, scientists, skilled workers and so on. The universities remained old-fashioned well into the next century, as did most of the grammar schools. (Until 1840 an endowed grammar school could not *legally* introduce modern subjects, though many did so illegally. The Head of Bedford School, who died in 1739, described his work as 'catechising nouns and pronouns eight hours every day'. At Bristol Grammar School science entered the curriculum as a 'voluntary extra' in 1868!) Some charity schools were organised under Church of England and nonconformist guidance, giving chiefly elementary education of a narrow kind—the catechism, knitting, spinning, writing and arithmetic—partly out of fear of the 'little dirty infantry which swarms up and down the alleys and lanes with curses and ribaldry in their mouths', as Marchamont Needham wrote in 1663. Gouge's scheme, in 1674, was mainly to teach poor Welsh children 'to read our English Bibles and treatises', and Firmin's School of Industry, 1675, was hardly distinguishable from child-labour, for it admitted children at three years and by five they were earning money by spinning at school. These charity schools failed to provide a general elementary education. They were greeted enthusiastically by Addison and Isaac Watts, but they declined rapidly after the reign of George I. (The narrow piety and niggardliness of this education might be contrasted with the 'justice' provided for the lower classes. In 1711–14 an unmarried mother was awarded 1s. 6d. per week towards maintenance of her child, but people were fined 8s. for swearing four oaths, 3s. 4d. for playing cricket on a Sunday, and £5 for shooting one partridge.)

The most hopeful developments appeared outside the established educational system. In a few private academies organised by Freemasons modern subjects were introduced, and this sometimes happened in the numerous Dissenting Academies which began as early as 1662, a direct result of the Restoration reaction to Puritanism. These institutions were designed to safeguard the Puritan religious content of education and ensure a strict moral code, but until 1690 the main study remained the classics, Latin was the language of instruction, and science was quite exceptional. (The second Newington Green Academy, where Samuel Wesley senior and Daniel Defoe were educated, was unusual, with its laboratory equipped with air pumps and thermometers, and at Sheriffhales one revolutionary teacher actually introduced essay writing *in English*.) After 1691 more modernisation took place, but it must not be exaggerated: only eight out of fifty-six academies are known to have introduced modern subjects before 1750.

And so the Restoration period, which Dryden sometimes praised to the skies for its literary and scientific achievements, failed dismally to respond to the urgent educational needs of the day or to heed the proposals of its advanced thinkers. Towards the end of the century his schoolmate John Locke turned his back upon both the old-fashioned system and plans for democratic schooling and advocated the education of gentlemen by individual tutors. Pope, who was privately educated, and Swift, who upheld the university classical curriculum, co-operated to satirise new educational ideas in their *Memoirs of . . . Martinus Scriblerus*. In particular they made fun of practical, as opposed to book, learning methods. Martin's father gives him modern playthings 'such as might prove of any benefit to his mind, by instilling an early notion of the sciences. For example, he found that marbles taught him percussion and the laws of motion; nutcrackers the use of the lever . . . and tops the centrifugal motion. . . . He never gave him a fig or an orange, but he obliged him to give an account from what country it came.'

So when we speak of Dryden's 'conservatism', one of the things this implies is his admiration for the classical education he received at Westminster School under Dr. Busby, and at Cambridge. He sent his sons to Westminster and seemed uninterested in the grave national problem of modernising an antiquated educational system. Whereas his fellow-student, Samuel Pepys, became governor of the famous school, Christ's Hospital, and tried strenuously to improve its curriculum, Dryden seemed aloof from such vital questions. Dryden, like most poets of the day, received a classical education in which the masterpieces of Greece and Rome were subjected to intense linguistic analysis, or were imitated in prose and verse; so we are not surprised to find that the poetry of the century is impregnated with classical ideas, myths and style. Dryden's most monumental work, which crowned the last years of his life, was his translation of Virgil's *Aeneid*, and this in its turn moulded 18th-century poetry, in particular popularising the *poetic diction* which became the stale hallmark of thousands of lines of verse. A large amount of Dryden's output consists of versions of Homer, Horace, Persius, Juvenal, Lucretius, Ovid and Theocritus. His original poems are filled with classical allusions, and he staged his own versions of plays by Sophocles and Plautus. Even where classical literature itself does not provide the content of a poem, or the allusions, the dignified style of Dryden recalls Virgil, and the habit of *making allusions to other literature* is continued in the biblical background to *Absalom and Achitophel*, or the constant reference to stage-plays in *Mac Flecknoe*. His numerous verse letters to such people as the playwrights Congreve, Etherege, Granville, Southerne and Sir Robert Howard, rely heavily on allusions to their writings, and his poems to Dr. Charleton, the Earl of Roscommon or Henry Higden are all comments on their publications. There is something inbred about Dryden's work, which is partly due to the common classical education he could assume in his readers, and partly due to the intimate circle of friends with whom he shared his literary pleasures. It is rather paradoxical, in fact, that Dryden, the professional man-of-letters and Poet Laureate, wrote much of his impersonal, public poetry essentially within the old tradition of a gentleman writing for a small group of friends. (*Mac Flecknoe* circulated in manuscript, for instance, long before it was published.) Nearly all his original poems celebrated a friend or patron (ranging from King Charles to the composer Purcell), a score of epistles are addressed to personal friends, and most of the elegies and epitaphs are on people he knew. Even such a public poem as *Absalom and Achitophel* is partly directed to Charles, Monmouth and others, in person, with the hope that they will take John Dryden's good advice. In fact, one of Dryden's great achievements is his ability to make a private poem on, say, a rival dramatist or his kinsman John Driden, into something for us all to enjoy. Out of something 'occasional' he often makes something universal. Thus, a letter to Mr. Congreve becomes an essay in literary history; one to Dr. Charleton becomes an appraisal of English science; an ode on Miss Killigrew becomes a complex defence of poetry as a divine art.

And yet Dryden's education surely tended to narrow his interests. Political and religious controversy engaged him as it did many writers of the time, but reading and writing were a lifelong obsession, specially his craftsman's dedication to the technical improvement of the English language. I do not, of course, wish to denigrate a writer's interest in writing! Dryden's technical virtuosity and his literary criticism are the fruits of this absorption. His learning was considerable, especially in the classics and theology. But my impression is that Dryden read books about life, rather than experiencing it at first hand. What has Dryden to tell us about Nature, about human love, about the comical, poignant details of everyday life? He can translate Virgil's *Georgics* and *Pastorals* for us, where 'Amaryllis fills the shady groves' and on the altar Tityrus sacrifices 'the tender firstlings of my woolly breed', but of Marvell's or Herrick's English countryside there is little evidence. In the Heroic Plays human love is represented by rhetorical posturings or gloating sexual desire, and Dryden's religious poems are mainly polemical or argumentative. Nobody has ever felt emotionally or spiritually nearer to Christ through reading *Religio Laici* or *The Hind and the Panther*, and I daresay many Christians have grimaced at Dryden's reference to religious faith in terms of insurance and banking:

> Faith is the best insurer of thy bliss;
> The bank above must fail before the venture miss.

And whereas the diaries of Pepys or Evelyn, and the narratives of John Bunyan, teem with fascinating details of everyday life among many classes of society, Dryden rarely quits the world of ideas, of controversy, except to set a farcical scene for Shadwell's coronation, to suggest Charles's death-chamber, or to allude in his plays to aristocratic wenching exploits and middle-class indignation at them. Pepys tells us of parties, friendly visits, tiffs with Mrs. Pepys, flirtations with pretty girls in church, of state affairs and of seamen dying of hunger in the London streets, and both he and Bunyan unfold for us the variety of life among the middle and artisan classes. A bookish classical education and the scholastic disputing-matches still in vogue at Cambridge cannot be entirely responsible for Dryden's intellectual bent, or his lack of interest in the detail of contemporary life, but must surely have strengthened a natural inclination. And therefore the charge that Dryden's rational, if rhetorical, style and his attraction to arguing and persuading, excluded visual narrative effects and emotional intensity, has much truth in it. Again, we have only to try an *experiment* to see whether it is true. Read a love poem by Donne and compare it with a Dryden song. Put any of George Herbert's poems of inner spiritual conflict side by side with *Religio Laici*. Test Dryden's Virgilian pastorals against Marvell's panorama of Yorkshire country life in *Upon Appleton House*. We cannot, of course, assume that Dryden was not an emotional man nor that he could not respond to the countryside (in which, at the houses of friends, he spent a good deal of time writing his poems), but simply that personal emotion and Nature rarely figure in his verse. As he showed in his play *All for Love*, he was capable of describing romantic love in a distinctive, tender style quite different from the blend of bombast and irony which he regularly used in the Heroic Plays. His love poems were mainly songs written for a specific scene in a play, not personal confessions. (If he wrote any 'confessions' he may not have wished to publish them.) Perhaps the 'occasion' for a passionate love poem simply did not present itself. Marvell's superb *To his Coy Mistress* may have been provoked by a mistress who was coy: presumably Dryden's mistress, the actress Ann Reeves, was not! (Most love poems express unrequited passion, not the happiness of love fulfilled.)

The renewed interest in classical poetry, which the Renaissance period had excitedly discovered, might easily have faded after the Elizabethan intoxication with it. The Metaphysical poets almost ignored it, and the middle-class Puritans of the revolutionary years were highly suspicious of its pagan and erotic character, and often claimed that Hebrew literature was the only acceptable model for the Christian poet. Marvell, at one point, declared that all his poems would henceforth be fitting garlands for the head of Christ, and even Milton, whose work is soaked in classical lore, made Jesus spurn classical literature in *Paradise Regained*. When Dryden's contemporary (and literary opponent) Sir Richard Blackmore wrote his immense poem, *Creation*, in seven books, he explicitly rejected all 'ornaments of poetic elegance' from classical mythology. Indeed Dryden himself in 1693, in his essay on satire, pleaded for Christian epics and the use of guardian angels in them (instead of mythical gods). But the middle-class Puritans never cleansed their education of pagan classicism. Even the Dissenting Academies remained true to Greek and Latin, and so all the middle-class poets of the later 17th and the 18th centuries received a classical education. This, together with the unholy alliance of John Milton, Puritan creator of *Paradise Lost*, and John Dryden, Catholic translator of Virgil, ensured that neo-classicism would triumph, despite the suspicions of Puritans and the attacks by Modernists on everything Ancient (led frequently by the scientists). So the two great Christian poets of the 17th century were largely responsible for seducing the 18th century with pagan neo-classicism: hence Pope's *Homer* and his *Imitations of Horace*. But although Milton christianised the pagan epic, the Christian epic which Dryden pleaded for was written in prose by John Bunyan in his prison-cell (to which he had been confined by the government Dryden so ably supported).

3

Science Demands the Muse

Having said that Dryden received an old-fashioned education we must immediately add that he was very receptive to up-to-date ideas, and in particular those associated with Thomas Hobbes, and the Royal Society (to which Hobbes was opposed). Hobbes, mathematical tutor to Charles II, delighted free-thinking (and rakish) courtiers and scandalised Christians by his book *Leviathan* (1651) and other works, in which he persuasively presented the materialistic view that the entire universe is *matter in motion*, including human thought and emotion, and that good and evil are merely moralising cant for man's desires and hates. (Imagination, for instance, is but 'decaying sense'.) Hobbes prudently disguised his atheistic materialism in religious terminology, but this did not fool his opponents. His philosophy led him to favour a political state, eternally valid, founded upon an unchanging contract between ruler and ruled. Hobbes, like Sigmund Freud in our day, was understood by the few, and misrepresented by the many. The libertines welcomed Hobbes because they thought he asserted that only sensations were real, and man should give free rein to his appetites. The royalists welcomed Hobbes because he seemed to give support to strong government and the *status quo*. Sceptics welcomed his materialism; and his attitude to thought, imagination and words encouraged some scientists, early psychologists and writers. It is not possible here to analyse in detail Dryden's debt to Hobbes, whose phrases he constantly quotes. In the last year of his life an aside about a Hobbist notion comes quite naturally: 'In the meantime, to follow the thread of my discourse (as thoughts, according to Mr. Hobbes, have always some connexion) . . .' Of course, Dryden might have used

Hobbist ideas and phrases in the same unthinking way that we talk about 'superiority complexes' and 'sublimation', but it is clear that the motivation of character and the interest in basic human appetites in the Heroic Plays owe much to Hobbist notions. Dryden did not of course need to read *Leviathan* to become interested in sex, but I think Hobbist ideas are behind his obsession with sexual sensations and the analytical way his characters constantly scrutinise their own feelings. Here is but one example of this, when Aureng-Zebe, in the play of that name, both surrenders to, and comments expressively upon, love in terms of physical sensations:

> Love mounts, and rolls about my stormy mind,
> Like fire, that's borne by a tempestuous wind.
> Oh, I could stifle you with eager haste!
> Devour your kisses with my hungry taste!
> Rush on you! eat you! wander o'er each part,
> Raving with pleasure, snatch you to my heart!
> Then hold you off, and gaze! then, with new rage
> Invade you, till my conscious limbs presage
> Torrents of joy, which all their banks o'erflow!
> So lost, so blessed, as I but then could know!

I don't think anybody had ever said anything quite like that on the stage before. Is it a serious Hobbist portrait of man the sensual animal, or is it satirical? Well, critics disagree on this point, but I merely wished to show how Dryden's poetry was inspired by the exhilarating, or menacing, new ideas that were in the air. Or was it? Unfortunately the critic who wants to put Dryden *in perspective* (in this case relating his ideas to those of Hobbes) has frankly to reveal that the above speech may just as well have been inspired by the Fourth Book of Lucretius, which Dryden himself translated:

> Our hands pull nothing from the parts they strain,
> But wander o'er the lovely limbs in vain.
> Nor when the youthful pair more closely join,
> When hands in hands they lock, and thighs in thighs they twine,
> Just in the raging foam of full desire,
> When both press on, both murmur, both expire,

They grip, they squeeze, their humid tongues they dart,
As each would force their way to t'other's heart . . .

The influence of the Royal Society was also a lasting one,
although its direct effect can most easily be detected in his early
work. This famous scientific body, membership of which is
still the highest honour for a scientist, was granted its charter in
1662, but it developed out of meetings in Oxford from 1645, and
at Gresham College from 1659. Many of the leading fellows were
connected with Puritanism in one way or another. (Wilkins, its
secretary, was Cromwell's brother-in-law; Walter Pope was
Wilkins's half-brother; Boyle, famed for his 'law', was educated
at Calvinist Geneva; Sprat, its historian, wrote an elegy on
Cromwell as Dryden had done.) Other celebrated figures
included Robert Hooke (1635–1703), outstanding physicist and
chemist, and presumably Dryden's schoolfellow at Westminster;
Christopher Wren, the architect; Seth Ward, astronomer;
Isaac Barrow, mathematician; John Wallis, author of an English
grammar; Nehemiah Grew, botanist; Sir William Petty,
statistician and educational reformer; Henry More the poet and
Cambridge Platonist; Joseph Glanvill, a most ardent defender of
the belief in witchcraft; the diarists Pepys and Evelyn; and the
poets Thomas Stanley, Thomas Flatman, Waller, Cowley and
John Dryden. The history of the Society is rather complicated for
it had to defend itself against wits like Samuel Butler, who
accused the virtuosos (as they were nicknamed) of being foolish
dabblers in nonsensical experiments (like Sir Nicholas Gimcrack
in Shadwell's play *The Virtuoso*, 1676), and against religious
critics who accused it variously of being Puritan, Roman
Catholic or atheistic—all good sticks to beat a dog with at this
period. In addition the Society was internally divided over its
principles; some scientists followed the lead of Descartes and
wished to deduce the nature of the world from his mathematical
theories, whereas others put their trust in the experimental
methods outlined by Bacon.

The Royal Society, and the countless amateur scientists, from
King Charles down, who installed laboratories in their houses,

were easy targets for the satirists. Samuel Butler's *The Elephant in the Moon* told how a scientist's lunar discovery was really due to a mouse that had got into his telescope. In the 18th century, when dilettante science was at its peak, Swift devoted a whole section of *Gulliver's Travels* to absurd experiments at the Academy of Lagado—one remembers the man who 'had been eight years upon a project for extracting sunbeams out of cucumbers, which were put into vials hermetically sealed, and let out to warm the air in raw inclement summers'. (Of course *we* dare not laugh too loudly, because one morning we shall open our newspapers and find that some scientist in Russia or America is actually doing this!) But the writers who supported science praised the experimental work; were optimistic about miraculous inventions which would improve the lot of mankind; damned Aristotle, Ptolemaic astronomy, and medieval word-spinning scholastics; and tried to *experiment* themselves with new scientific imagery and scientific subjects. Cowley wrote his ode *To the Royal Society*, declaring that Bacon had, like Moses, led us to the 'promised land'. Davenant's voluminous epic *Gondibert* included a lengthy, enraptured tour of a science museum, though the style is unfortunately museum-dry:

Next it, a whale is high in cables tied,
Whose strength might herds of elephants control,
Then all (in pairs of every kind) they spied,
Which death's wreck leaves, of fishes, beast, and fowl.

(This is the quatrain-form which Dryden borrowed for *Annus Mirabilis*.) Thomas Flatman, F.R.S., wrote a poem against the superstitions of astrology; J. Moore was later to write about fen-drainage and Yalden to pen neo-classical rhetoric on the dangers of coal-mining, but the truth is that very little poetry was directly inspired by science in its early stages. Later on the optical theories of Newton inspired a veritable spate of poems, but the really 'scientific' poems of any magnitude appeared only in the next century. Thomson's *The Seasons* (1726 to 1730), in grandiose Miltonic blank verse, presents a fascinating scientific panorama of Nature, from sublime Newtonian descriptions of rainbows to up-to-date advice on sheep-dipping and insecticides—he had to keep correcting his poem when better ones were invented. This is how Thomson speaks of flowers greeting the sunlight—they await

> . . . the morning beam, to give to light,
> Raised through ten thousand different plastic tubes,
> The balmy treasures of the former days.

The other long and serious scientific poem is Blackmore's *Creation*, a huge versified treatise on everything. A brief passage on human digestive processes will indicate how near to the scientific textbook poetry had come:

> The mouth, with proper faculties endued,
> First entertains, and then divides the food;
> Two adverse rows of teeth the meat prepare,
> On which the glands fermenting juice confer;
> Nature has various tender muscles placed,
> By which the artful gullet is embraced;
> Some the long funnel's curious mouth extend,
> Through which ingested meats with ease descend;
> Other confederate pairs for nature's use
> Contract the fibres, and the twitch produce,
> Which gently pushes on the grateful food
> To the wide stomach, by its hollow road . . .

(This may have seemed as novel and as fascinating to the contemporary reader as James Kirkup's account of a surgical operation, *A Correct Compassion*, does to us.)

Dryden, as we have seen, was a Fellow of the Royal Society from the start (though inexplicably he failed to pay his dues and was ejected in 1666). He specifically praised the Society in *Annus Mirabilis*, published in 1667, and in 1664 he had been elected to the committee for improving the English language. In 1663 his poem *To my honoured Friend Dr. Charleton* was prefixed to the latter's *Chorea Gigantum*, in which the Royal Fellow demolished Inigo Jones's thesis that Stonehenge was the remains of a Roman temple. Charleton believed that the Danes had erected the stones as a place where they would elect their king. (This afforded

Dryden the nice opportunity to compare Charleton's restoring the Danish kings to Stonehenge with the restoration of Charles to his throne, and some critics interpret this poem as chiefly political in intent.) Dryden begins with the usual 'scientific' denigration of Aristotle (the Stagirite), whose tyrannical authority had to be broken:

> The longest tyranny that ever swayed
> Was that wherein our ancestors betrayed
> Their free-born Reason to the Stagirite,
> And made his torch their universal light.

He celebrates the achievements of English scientists, including Gilbert's work on magnetism and Harvey's discovery of the circulation of the blood:

> The world to Bacon does not only owe
> Its present knowledge, but its future too.
> Gilbert shall live, till lodestones cease to draw
> Or British fleets the boundless ocean awe.
>
> . . . .
> The circling streams, once thought but pools, of blood
> (Whether life's fuel or the body's food)
> From dark oblivion Harvey's name shall save;
> While Ent keeps all the honour that he gave.

As poetry this is unremarkable—a catalogue of names, a little wit, and meagre information. Sir George Ent, physician, who in 1641 vindicated Harvey's discoveries, gets a vaguely phrased mention. After eulogising Charleton's medical and archeological talents Dryden finishes on a note of praise for Charles's restoration, deftly reminding us that Prince Charles had found time to visit Stonehenge after the defeat at the Battle of Worcester:

> These ruins sheltered once his sacred head,
> Then when from Worcester's fatal field he fled;
> Watched by the genius of this royal place,
> And mighty visions of the Danish race,
> His refuge then was for a temple shown:
> But, he restored, 'tis now become a throne.

Even in this poem politics seems to be more important to Dryden than science.

In 1674 Dryden can still assert: 'A man should be learned in several sciences, and should have a reasonable, philosophical, and in some measure a mathematical head, to be a complete and excellent poet . . .' but after his conversion to Catholicism both science and Hobbes's materialism seem decisively rejected:

Rest then, my soul, from endless anguish freed;
Nor sciences thy guide, nor sense thy creed.

But in a more indirect fashion science did continue to influence Dryden's poetry. Among the things scientists wanted to improve was the English language itself. Sprat thought that practical crafts and the scientific investigation of nature would provide new technical terms, imagery and similes. (Dryden collected ship-repair terms for *Annus Mirabilis* and gave a history of navigation, but as he grew older he abandoned such experiments and preferred elegant language. When he translated Virgil for his middle-class readers he scorned to render *mollis amaracus* as *sweet marjoram* for it was one of 'those village words'.) But the main demand of the Royal Society was for a simple, plain style— 'a close, naked, natural way of speaking; positive expressions; clear senses; a native easiness; bringing all things as near the mathematical plainness, as they can . . .' We have only to read a page from the prose of Donne, Milton or Sir Thomas Browne and compare it with the new style of Dryden's essays and (later) Defoe's, Fielding's and Richardson's novels, or Addison's essays, to realise that a revolution in prose-style happened during Dryden's lifetime, and a modern, standard prose was born. The influences were social as well as scientific, and the growing 'rational religion' of the period was also accompanied by plain, rational sermons. (Compare, for instance, sermons by John Donne with those by Isaac Barrow, F.R.S.) And so Dryden's early enthusiasm for science could at least have encouraged his search for a simpler, more direct style. He abandoned the metaphysical conceit (though he always retained wit), simplified his syntax, perfected the couplet (where the reader assimilates the

35

poem in two-line doses), adopted the standard vocabulary of his educated reader, and aimed at a persuasive clarity in his prosaic, argumentative verse. Other features of his poetry—satirical simplification, psychological analysis of characters, the public significance of his themes, the didactic tones and so on—are all part of a general movement during the second half of the century, in which a new kind of social literature was being developed, responsive to the middle-class, commercial society which was appearing. Science was one of the pervasive forces in this society and, directly or indirectly, it helped to mould the literature of the age. In fact, 18th-century humanists such as Pope and Swift felt the dehumanising power of science to be so strong that they openly attacked science in their writing. And it may well be, as C. J. Horne has argued, that the Augustan cult of classical mythology and the device of personification was an 'attempt to keep up some human warmth among the depersonalising forces of science'. It is significant that when William Blake raised the Romantic flag of individualism and emotion he first made a ferocious attack on Newtonian science.

And so if we consider Dryden's political satires, his discursive religious poems, his assured comments on the great figures of his day in panegyrics, odes, epistles or elegies, his verse-journalism, his tributes to poets, painters and composers, his labours to present the classical world of Virgil as a model to his countrymen, his strenuous attempt to improve literature and literary taste by his critical essays, we can see that the notion of *order*, of conserving and gradually improving, is fundamental to his entire life and work. The more we read him, the more we are convinced that the traditional picture of the political and religious turncoat is wrong. Dryden had his human imperfections and his interests were limited, but the modern perspective tends to view Dryden as a consistent upholder of the values in which he believed. His basic desire was for order—political, religious, literary. His basic fear was of anarchy. Civil war or attacks upon the constitutional monarchy, fanatical sects, or Shadwellian dullness, spelled for him anarchy. Order therefore he found in the King, the Church and the Classics.

Of course, life defies our neat formulations, as Dryden discovered. Defending the rights of the constitutional monarch led him into Tory partisanship—into that civil strife which was his constant fear. Moreover, during King William's reign, Dryden had logically to continue his allegiance to the exiled, Catholic monarch, James II: royalist obedience to the ousted king meant potential sedition against the *de facto* reigning one. Should he now put 'civil peace' before principles, as he had perhaps done when the usurper Cromwell had ruled? Similarly, John Dryden the Anglican could find order in a national church, headed by a Protestant sovereign, and thus dismiss with amusement or fear the anarchy of dissenting fanatics. Roman Catholic John Dryden could still support the legal Catholic monarch with conscience, but now his religious views endangered the order provided by a national church. And when an 'illegal' Protestant is on the throne, Dryden himself is one of the minority which threatens the public peace. And in the field of literature Dryden was faced with similar contradictions. If you put your faith in classical rules, then you have to demote Shakespeare for breaking them. If you model your writing upon the public modes of the pagan classics is there not a danger that your panegyrics, satires, odes, epistles and elegies will add a false gloss of elegance and virtue to men and to a society which fall far below the ideal your poetry paints? (Like the beautiful classical drapery and the flattering improvements which neo-classical painters introduced, the neo-classical ornaments and devices could create the illusion of 'order', of civilised refinement, instead of naturalistically telling the truth about society. It is true that satire exposes the villains and the fops, but in Dryden's satires 'dullness' and Achitophel are so decisively defeated that 'order' seems invincible.) All these are complex matters, which arise because we are looking at Dryden in his context—which, after all, is as wide and as profound as life itself. And life, it seems to me, refused to be bound by Dryden's rather static concept of order. Time and time again Dryden diagnosed the ills of his day as a simple revolt of the people against the king, which for him mirrored Adam's revolt against God. Everywhere, in poems, in plays and in prose, he alluded to this basic conception. The question for us is: are we satisfied with this key to the riddle of the universe? It dominated Dryden's thought. Milton wrote an enormous poem on the theme of 'man's first disobedience'. Thomas Hobbes's key to disorder was mankind's 'perpetual and restless desire of power'. Today's thinkers offer us other keys to understanding our universe—Freud's concept of the *libido*, Marx's concept of *class-struggle*, the existentialist concept of *choice*—which we may measure against Dryden's concept of *rebellion*. And so, studying a poet in perspective leads us to ask fundamental questions about life, and to re-examine our own beliefs. One reason why Dryden is worth reading is because he provokes us to think.

4

Verse Technique: The Heroic Couplet

We have seen how science, an aspect of the context in which Dryden's poetry grew, had a specific influence on vocabulary, style and subject-matter. May we then assume that even the minute details of literary works are connected, openly or in a hidden way, with the vast background of history, society and ideas? At least this possibility raises many fascinating questions. We wonder why different literary forms became popular in different periods. Why does the novel appear only with the rise to importance of the middle classes? Why cannot poets write epics today? Why did the Elizabethans produce tragedies but the Victorians melodramas? Why are periods of great drama so very brief? And so we could continue, and become more and more aware that literary history does have its own stages of development, which may correspond to stages in an evolving social culture.

Even if we consider something relatively narrow, such as verse technique, we can also see distinct stages of development. We think of such characteristic features as medieval ballads, Elizabethan blank verse and sonnets, the Metaphysical conceit, Caroline and Restoration lyrics, the later 17th-century vogue for Pindaric odes, the Augustan heroic couplet, the Romantic ballad, the Victorian 'long poem', 20th-century free verse. These are only certain dominant features, of course; there are always exceptions (as, for example, Thomson's blank verse Nature poem in a period usually considered favourable to urban verse in heroic couplets). So perhaps we could here look at the heroic couplet, which Dryden took, experimented with, and made into a subtle verse form, eminently suitable for Pope and the Augustans to use and polish still more finely.

The so-called heroic couplet is simply two rhyming lines of five iambic feet, making ten syllables. The iambic pattern of a weak stress, followed by a strong stress, is the basis of normal speech—English being a stressed language in which the iambic pattern naturally develops. The verse foot may be reversed (*strong* : *weak*), or we may have *strong* : *strong*, or *weak* : *weak* : *strong*, or *strong* : *weak* : *weak*—in other words, trochee, spondee, anapaest and dactyl; but many modern writers on metre have the welcome habit of regarding all these merely as *variations* on the basic iambic metre. This is not just a glib bit of prosody-without-tears but the realisation that the English norm seems to be iambic—in fact, it is so natural that we are hardly aware of this beat, in verse or in ordinary speech. Only when there is a variation, anapaestic, dactylic, etc., are we immediately conscious of *metre*.

Blank verse consists of the same ten-syllable iambic line, without the rhymes, and therefore the sense can be extended to as many lines as desired. The opening sentence of *Paradise Lost* spreads sinuously over sixteen syntactically elaborate lines:

> Of man's first disobedience, and the fruit
> Of that forbidden tree, whose mortal taste
> Brought death into the world, and all our woe,
> With loss of Eden, till one greater man
> Restore us, and regain the blissful seat,
> Sing heavenly Muse, that on the secret top
> Of Oreb, or of Sinai, didst inspire
> That shepherd, who first taught the chosen seed,
> In the beginning how the heavens and earth
> Rose out of chaos: or if Sion hill
> Delight thee more, and Siloa's brook that flowed
> Fast by the oracle of God; I thence
> Invoke thy aid to my adventurous song,
> That with no middle flight intends to soar
> Above th'Aonian mount, while it pursues
> Things unattempted yet in prose or rhyme.

When Dryden, with Milton's permission, made a stage version of part of this epic, he used heroic couplets. Here is the first speech of the newly-created Adam (who, it seems, has read Dryden's contemporary, Descartes, for he rephrases his celebrated *Cogito ergo sum*—I think, therefore I am—as he reflects philosophically on himself, God and Nature):

> What am I? or from whence? For that I am,
> I know, because I think; but whence I came,
> Or how this frame of mine began to be,
> What other being can disclose to me?
> I move, I see; I speak, discourse, and know,
> Though now I am, I was not always so.
> Then that from which I was, must be before:
> Whom as my spring of being I adore.
> How full of ornament is all I view
> In all its parts! and seems as beautiful as new:
> O goodly ordered work! O power divine!
> Of thee I am; and what I am is thine!

In the Elizabethan play, blank verse proved the ideal, flexible instrument for complex rhetoric, formal speeches of kings, witty argument, and colloquial conversation. Where necessary extra syllables were added, to dilute the effect of verse, and the result is often indistinguishable from prose. The transformation of blank verse into rhyming couplets immediately tends to make the basic unit two lines. There is still no limit to the length of the poem, which is not divided therefore into sections of a regular size, as it is when stanzas are employed. Instead the poem can split into paragraphs, of varying lengths, as dictated by the subject-matter. Sense and sentences can be allowed to overflow from one couplet to the next, but the usual tendency will be for the matter to be fed to the reader in two-line spoonfuls—a fairly easy way to assimilate something, but not always as satisfying as a good, steady drink. In other words, the couplet-form (especially the end-stopped type, where the sense is not allowed to overflow) encourages the writer to present his material in disparate bits, to reduce a complex experience to short, single statements, to compress large topics into the two-line unit. So an analytical approach to experience, or a piecemeal, brick-by-brick accumulation of detail, or the economical generalisation, all seem to be naturally associated with the heroic couplet. As there is so much to be done in each couplet, the poet must take great pains about its internal organisation, packing the ideas as neatly as possible into the confined space. But a standard packing technique becomes boring after scores of similar lines, and so there is the constant search for variety.

If you have only two lines to manipulate, you have to be very sensitive to minute variations in stress, balance of phrases, word order, vowel and consonant music, alliteration, vocabulary contrasts, rhythms, etc. You can contrast line one with line two. You can split the line into two balancing phrases, like a see-saw. You can spit it out, word after word, a stress on each one. You can lumber along on spondees or trip along on anapaests. To analyse all the technical details of Dryden's heroic couplets would really require a computer, and I do not think that one can usefully absorb the sort of descriptive analysis exemplified by the following remark (about Dryden's verse): 'In most of the examples an unaccented final syllable of a polysyllable is followed by an unemphatic article in a normally stressed position, which in turn is followed by an adjective (which if monosyllabic may be emphatic, and if polysyllabic may carry secondary accent); and a syllable in stressed position concludes the variation.' Personally I have found that actual *examples* of complex technique help much more to make one sensitive to minute verbal devices, and that the most effective and enjoyable way of discovering the secrets of any verse-form is to write imitations of the poet one is studying. This is what John Dryden did at Westminster School. Write ten lines of Shakespearian blank verse and five Drydenian heroic couplets, and a score of 'technical devices' will suddenly become intimately alive for you. You do not have to take my word for this: again, take a cue from the 17th century and *experiment*.

We can learn more about the heroic couplet and Dryden's achievements by putting him in the historical perspective—that is, seeing him as part of the history of the form. So we will have a quick glance at the couplet from Chaucer to Pope. Chaucer often makes the sense flow expansively through the couplet, but more typically he uses the two-line (or even one-line) unit as the appropriate form for his apparently random, odds-and-ends of description, disarmingly casual. Here is his quick eye and mind scanning the Wife of Bath:

A good Wif was ther of biside Bathe,
But she was somdel deef, and that was scathe . . .
Hir coverchiefs ful fyne were of ground;
I dorste swere they weyeden ten pound
That on a Sunday weren upon hir heed.
Hir hosen weren of fyn scarlet reed,
Ful streite yteyd, and shoes ful moyste and newe.
Boold was her face, and fair and reed of hewe.
She was a worthy woman al hir lyve:
Housbondes at chirche dore she hadde fyve . . .

Now we jump the centuries to John Donne's satirical portrait of a court gossip, in which he deliberately flouts the couplet's natural discipline:

                              . . . He knows
When the queen frowned, or smiled, and he knows what
A subtle statesman may gather of that;
He knows who loves; whom; and who by poison
Hastes to an office's reversion;
He knows who hath sold his land, and now does beg
A licence, old iron, boots, shoes, and egg-
Shells to transport; shortly boys shall not play
At span-counter, or blow-point, but they pay
Toll to some courtier; and wiser than all us,
He knows what lady is not painted; thus
He with home-meats tries me; I belch, spew, spit,
Look pale, and sickly, like a patient; yet
He thrusts on more . . .

The erratic bursts of phrase mirror the gesticulating court gossip's chatter and the listener's pent annoyance. The jerky rhythms act on the reader's nerves and re-enact the scene, but at the same time comment ironically upon it. Donne is exploiting all the freedom and variety found in blank verse, with wonderful ingenuity, and cocking a snook at the strict couplet form—as we

see from his impudent fun with the eggshells, which he cracks
neatly on the rim of the couplet.

Waller and Denham were repeatedly praised by the Augustans
for refining English verse, but we regard them today as minor
poets. Waller's *A Panegyric to my Lord Protector* (1655) employed
heroic couplets, in contrast to Dryden's quatrains on the same
subject. (The quatrain merely takes two couplets, rearranges the
rhymes into alternating a-b-a-b, and thereby produces a
compact little stanza, familiar to us in Gray's celebrated elegy.)
Waller's poem moves the caesura (or sense-break) rather obviously back and forth within the line, and he too neatly chops
his material into balanced, opposing segments. But how amazing
this methodical splicing must have sounded to ears accustomed to
Donne's spasmodic slish-slashing:

> Your never-failing sword made war to cease,
> And now you heal us with the arts of peace,
> Our minds with bounty, and with awe engage,
> Invite affection, and restrain our rage:
> Less pleasure take, brave minds in battle won,
> Than in restoring such as are undone,
> Tigers have courage, and the rugged bear,
> But man alone can, whom he conquers, spare.
> To pardon willing, and to punish loth,
> You strike with one hand, but you heal with both . . .

The formal support of the rhymes and the internal balance can be
appreciated if the last two lines are rearranged in normal word-
order:

> Willing to pardon, and loth to punish,
> You strike with one hand, but you heal with both . . .

In the *Imitating Mr. Waller* poem, you might ask whether
'Willing to pardon, yet to punish loth' would be an improvement
on the original, as it puts 'willing' and 'loth' at opposite ends of the
see-saw. Also 'willing to pardon' mirrors the speedy willingness
of Cromwell, whereas 'to pardon willing' seems stiff and reluc-
tant. These are the sort of things to which you become sensitive

when you are practising writing instead of merely listening to critics.

Denham's most famous poem was *The Thames from Cooper's Hill* (1643) which appears very banal now. The last four lines were excessively praised, imitated, alluded to and parodied:

> O could I flow like thee, and make thy stream
> My great example, as it is my theme!
> Though deep, yet clear, though gentle, yet not dull,
> Strong without rage, without o'er-flowing full.

Perhaps it was the implied golden-mean balance of emotion and control, 'strong without rage', that appealed to the emerging Augustan sensibility. As the date shows, the heroic couplet was not an 18th-century invention, but the neater, often end-stopped, forms were only one of several trends in the 17th century. Milton's *At a Vacation Exercise* (1645) glides smoothly over the line-ends as though it were unrestricted blank verse:

> Such where the deep transported mind may soar
> Above the wheeling poles, and at heaven's door
> Look in, and see each blissful deity
> How he before the thunderous throne doth lie,
> Listening to what unshorn Apollo sings
> To the touch of golden wires, while Hebe brings
> Immortal nectar to her kingly sire . . .

Crashaw, in his *Music's Duel* (1646), charges his fluid couplets with the throb and flow of the nightingale's song—an amazing achievement, but, like Donne's, obtained really by ignoring the innate characteristics of the couplet:

> Then starts she suddenly into a throng
> Of short thick sobs, whose thund'ring volleys float,
> And roll themselves over her lubric throat
> In panting murmurs, stilled out of her breast
> That ever-bubbling spring; the sugred nest
> Of her delicious soul, that there does lie
> Bathing in streams of liquid melody . . .

Here the exotic, expressive vocabulary hides the bare bones of the couplet, and similar effects are found in Dryden's Heroic Plays, especially where the emotion runs red-hot. But for rhapsodic flights Dryden usually turned to the flexible Pindaric ode—the period's equivalent of our free verse.

Many of Dryden's contemporaries used heroic couplets, and yet each has a distinctive tone. Andrew Marvell, ten years older than Dryden, developed some of the characteristic Augustan effects of the couplet—balance of phrase, end-stopping, and crescendo passages—but on the whole his lines are roughly strung together, mirroring the informality of coffee-house talk rather than the elegance of the drawing-room. This portrait of one of Charles II's mistresses, Barbara Villiers (known at various times in her notorious career as Mrs. Palmer, Countess of Castlemaine, and Duchess of Cleveland), also gives us a glimpse of a partisan poetry opposed to the royalist satires of Dryden:

> Paint Castlemaine in colours that will hold,
> Her, not her picture, for she now grows old.
> She through her lackey's drawers as he ran,
> Discerned love's cause, and a new flame began.
> Her wonted joys thenceforth and court she shuns,
> And still within her mind the footman runs:
> His brazen calves, his brawny thighs, (the face
> She slights) his feet shaped for a smoother race.
> Poring within her glass she re-adjusts
> Her looks, and oft-tried beauty now distrusts:
> Fears lest he scorn a woman once essayed,
> And now first, wished she ere had been a maid.
> Great love, how dost thou triumph, and how reign,
> That to a groom couldst humble her disdain!
> Stripped to her skin, see how she stooping stands,
> Nor scorns to rub him down with those fair hands;
> And washing (lest the scent her crime disclose)
> His sweaty hooves, tickles him 'twixt the toes.

It would be nice to know more of Dryden's attitude to Marvell, his colleague in the Cromwellian service, and during the Restoration the most pungent satirist of Charles and his ministers. In the preface to *Religio Laici* (1682), after Marvell's death, Dryden compared him to Martin Marprelate, 'the Marvell of those times . . . the first Presbyterian scribbler who sanctified libels and scurrility to the use of the good old cause'. Dryden would have been sympathetic, however, to another contemporary, Samuel Butler, whose anti-Puritan satire *Hudibras* was published in three parts (1663, 1664, 1678), to the delight of Charles and the court. Dryden's reactions to Butler's octosyllabic couplets and the comic two- and three-syllable rhymes show that he thought this measure fit for burlesque, but not for more serious satire, for which he preferred the greater dignity of heroic couplets: 'the shortness of his verse, and the quick returns of rhyme, had debased the dignity of style. And besides, the double rhyme . . . is not so proper for manly satire; for it turns earnest too much to jest, and gives us a boyish kind of pleasure . . .' As a contrast to Dryden's heroic couplets we may cite a few lines from *Hudibras*, which have a wonderful knock-about zest, and also reveal to us a common Restoration attitude to the Puritans:

> For his religion it was fit
> To match his learning and his wit:
> 'Twas Presbyterian true blue,
> For he was of that stubborn crew
> Of Errant Saints, whom all men grant
> To be the true Church Militant:
> Such as do build their faith upon
> The holy text of pike and gun;
> Decide all controversies by
> Infallible artillery;
> And prove their doctrine orthodox
> By apostolic blows and knocks;
> Call fire and sword and desolation,
> A godly-thorough-Reformation,
> Which always must be carried on,
> And still be doing, never done:
> As if religion were intended
> For nothing else but to be mended.

The Earl of Rochester, sometimes Dryden's patron, sometimes his enemy, often used heroic couplets to reproduce the world of fops and nymphs with sardonic wit, but in his more sombre poems, such as *A Satire against Mankind*, the emotionally-charged argument (a simplified, cynical version of Hobbes's teaching) employs couplets that have a force and clarity very like Dryden's, though the tone of disgust is more characteristic of Rochester:

> Which is the basest creature, man, or beast?
> Birds feed on birds, beasts on each other prey,
> But savage man alone, does man betray:
> Pressed by necessity, they kill for food,
> Man undoes man, to do himself no good.
> With teeth and claws, by Nature armed, they hunt
> Nature's allowances, to supply their want.
> But man, with smiles, embraces, friendship, praise,
> Inhumanly his fellows' life betrays;
> With voluntary pains, works his distress,
> Not through necessity, but wantonness.
> For hunger, or for love, they fight, or tear,
> Whilst wretched man is still in arms for fear;
> For fear he arms, and is of arms afraid,
> By fear, to fear, successively betrayed;
> Base fear, the source whence his best passions came,
> His boasted honour, and his dear bought fame.

Features such as the first half-line balanced against the second, or the catalogue ('with smiles, embraces, friendship, praise'), or the reversal of terms ('For fear he arms, and is of arms afraid'), etc., show that others besides Dryden were experimenting with the internal organisation of the couplet, concentrating our attention upon minute effects within one line, even within a phrase. The result is something much more meticulous, analytical, cerebral, disciplined than we have seen in the fluid couplets of Milton, Crashaw or Donne. The danger is that the strict, methodical organisation of rhythms, word-order, juxtapositions of phrases, balance, caesura-shifts, end-stopped rhymes, etc., will exclude such tonal effects as Crashaw's exhilaration (mainly due to vocabulary and enjambment), Milton's rhapsodic sweep, or Donne's witty eccentricity. Without their humorous venom Marvell's lines would be rather commonplace, and Rochester's philosophy-textbook discussion is only compelling because of the intense disgust which charges the stale, conventional diction ('works his distress', 'wretched man', or 'his best passions' are woefully drab). But when this internal discipline is matched with emotion, clarity of expression and an apt image, the unadventurous idiom is less harmful, as we see in these impressive lines by Rochester:

> Then old age, and experience, hand in hand,
> Lead him to death, and make him understand,
> After a search so painful, and so long,
> That all his life he has been in the wrong;
> Huddled in dirt, the reasoning engine lies,
> Who was so proud, so witty, and so wise.
> Merely for safety after fame we thirst,
> For all men would be cowards, if they durst.

John Oldham, to whom Dryden expressed a special debt (in his elegy upon his young friend), managed to combine Hudibrastic verbal buffoonery with the heroic couplet form, and though his staple line is, as Dryden remarked, harsh and rough enough, he did employ many of the devices which Dryden and Pope were to take and refine. Here is a good bit of anti-Catholic, rotten-egg pelting, produced simply by packing dozens of details, from the external rituals of Catholic devotion, higgledy-piggledy into a brief paragraph (and reminiscent of Milton's description of Catholic friars whirling about limbo like space-debris):

> Should I tell all their countless knaveries,
> Their cheats, and shams, and forgeries, and lies,
> Their cringing, crossings, censings, sprinklings, chrisms,
> Their conjurings, and spells, and exorcisms,
> Their motley habits, maniples and stoles,
> Albs, ammits, rochets, chimers, hoods, and cowls;
> Should I tell all their several services,
> Their trentals, masses, dirges, rosaries;
> Their solemn pomps, their pageants, and parades,
> Their holy masques, and spiritual cavalcades . . .

Dryden's attacks on Fanatics often have this custard-pie farce element, in which words are hurled joyously at the opponent's face. In fact one wonders whether Oldham's anti-Catholic fireworks were meant mainly to dazzle and amuse, and not as serious criticisms, just as our films and television programmes burlesque various fashionable Aunt Sallys (the Establishment, Culture, Communism, the Upper Classes, etc.) for the fun of it. Professional satirists, like professional journalists, are a hard-boiled lot, and one sometimes suspects that the literary guerrilla warfare they conducted provided them with a good deal of excitement.

Now that we have examined the heroic couplet in perspective we can see that Dryden worked within the trends of his own time. He consolidated many of the features he found in Waller, Marvell, Rochester, or Oldham, but though he refined the instrument it was left to Alexander Pope (1688–1744) to polish it more elegantly. We might glance at a few lines by Pope to see how he modified Dryden's work. Dryden, for example, had shown how a man who is a bundle of incongruities can be suit-ably mirrored in verses built with antitheses and word-catalogues:

> A man so various, that he seemed to be
> Not one, but all mankind's epitome.
> Stiff in opinions, always in the wrong;
> Was everything by starts, and nothing long:
> But, in the course of one revolving moon,
> Was chemist, fiddler, statesman and buffoon;
> Then all for women, painting, rhyming, drinking,
> Besides ten thousand freaks that died in thinking.

Pope, in his Sporus portrait, increases these rhythmic effects, which are intended to echo the volatile nature of Lord Hervey:

> Or at the ear of Eve, familiar toad!
> Half froth, half venom, spits himself abroad,
> In puns, in politics, or tales, or lies,
> Or spite, or smut, or rhymes, or blasphemies.
> His wit all see-saw, between that and this,
> Now high, now low, now master up, now miss,
> And he himself one vile antithesis.

Dryden sometimes adds couplets together to form a paragraph, but Pope makes this into a rhythmic crescendo effect. In the following passage there is a mock-heroic rhetoric, in which the mounting climax of the rhythm climbs parallel with an increasing absurdity or wickedness in the character portrayed, ending in an explosive antithesis which bursts the mock-heroic pose:

> See how the world its veterans rewards!
> A youth of frolics, an old age of cards;
> Fair to no purpose, artful to no end,
> Young without lovers, old without a friend;
> A fop their passion, but their prize a sot,
> Alive, ridiculous, and dead, forgot!

Pope uses a host of devices, which are hardly developed at all by Dryden, and we may briefly refer to them in passing. There is the *pun*:

> None need a guide, by sure attraction led,
> And strong impulsive *gravity* of head . . .

Zeugma—the use of one verb with two highly unrelated nouns. Here the effect is to suggest that neither the woman's virtue nor her costume are stain-resistant:

> Or stain her honour, or her new brocade.

The *catalogue with one disparate element* suggests that Belinda values equally the scriptures and her cosmetics. On her table lie:

> Puffs, powders, patches, bibles, billet-doux.

An *antithesis* can be evaluative, forcing the reader to equate both terms:

> A hero perish, or a sparrow fall.

The *allusive phrase* can be deliberately inappropriate, so that here it recalls a background of sane values (as in a river):

> And the fresh vomit run for ever green.

These examples can only hint at the meticulous craftsmanship of Pope, who went much further than Dryden in technical subtlety and minute effects of irony—though something of Dryden's earthy vigour and breezy gusto was lost in the process.

Aspects of Dryden's technical brilliance will be seen when groups of poems are studied in detail, and his voluminous verse translations contain hundreds of lines of stylistic virtuosity— one should at least glance at the Sixth Satire from Juvenal, the First Book of Ovid's *Art of Love*, the Ninth Ode of the First Book of Horace, and the versions of Lucretius. Only a few lines of the Second Part of *Absalom and Achitophel* are by Dryden, but they include this hilarious passage on Shadwell, the drunken, tun-bellied Og of this portrait:

> Now stop your noses, Readers, all and some,
> For here's a tun of midnight work to come,
> Og from a treason tavern rolling home.
> Round as a globe, and liquored every chink,
> Goodly and great he sails behind his link;
> With all this bulk there's nothing lost in Og,
> For every inch that is not fool is rogue:
> A monstrous mass of foul corrupted matter,
> As all the devils had spewed to make the batter.
> When wine has given him courage to blaspheme,
> He curses God, but God before cursed him . . .
> The midwife laid her hand on his thick skull,
> With this prophetic blessing—*Be thou dull* . . .

Much of the force of these lines comes from the vocabulary— globe, bulk, mass, matter, batter, thick skull—which suggests size, weight and density (physical and mental), and so presents and criticises Shadwell at the same time. The couplet form encourages strong, one-line statements, each one a heavy thud— note how many monosyllabic words there are, and the high ratio of consonants to vowels. 'Og . . . rolling home round as a globe' has a nice succession of o's as rotund as Shadwell himself, and the clotted jumble of consonants in 'monstrous mass of foul corrupted matter' adds to the revolting notion of batter made of vomit. The verbal horseplay is controlled by the witty comments, as in the crushing repartee of: 'He curses God, but God before cursed him.'

We can only study brief samples of Dryden's technique in detail, but once we have done this with a few passages, our sensitivity to minute effects is rapidly increased, and our minds, more alert, read with keener enjoyment. This is the reason why we scrutinise technical devices—not to attach ponderous Latin names to them, but to taste with finer palates the feast of words.

In the poem on Oldham, for instance (which is discussed in the chapter on elegies), Dryden's kindly criticism of Oldham's rough technique is completed *in the poem itself* by a demonstration of how to write well! Let us here note only one technical device— the art of gradation, of tiny modifications. Thus, Dryden's relationship with Oldham is initially expressed rather tentatively: 'began to think and call my own'. Then this is strengthened with: 'near allied', and finally is cemented by the assertive words: 'same ... common ... alike ... same'. There is nothing spectacular in the vocabulary. The gradual friendship, ending in identity of interest, is carefully, imperceptibly *mirrored in the technique*. Similarly we could note the slight but significant variations in terms to suggest nuances: too little—too lately; think—call; performed—won; ripe—abundant; advancing—added; maturing—mellows—sweets. Or again, see how one word shades into another: *own* into *allied*; *poetic* into *lyre*; *goal* into *race*; *performed* into *ripe*; *rugged* into *force*; *error* into *betrayed*. With sly tact Dryden shows how Oldham's crude verse could have been made more subtle. When he speaks of the 'dull sweets of rhyme' he *illustrates* the cloying effect by putting the thought into a triplet (three rhyming lines) ending with *prime*, *time* and *rhyme*.

'Should one really put a poem under a microscope like this?' I can hear an exasperated reader ask. Why not? You never know what you might discover. And again I appeal to the notion of *experiment*. If the revelation according to the microscope results in renewed enthusiasm or greater sensitivity, surely it has proved its value. If it does not, try using a telescope (I mean, viewing the poem as a whole). These are all very good 17th-century instruments, as are the thermometer, barometer, and air pump, not to mention Denis Papin's pressure-cooker, a primitive magic-lantern, blood transfusion apparatus, an automatic loom, and a machine for composing music. Dryden, who for years collected material for a scientific work on prosody, was intensely interested in the minute details of his craft. I see no reason why we should not share his fascination with technique—if we wish. On the other hand, each reader is free to read poetry in whatever way he likes—even with the Claude glass! (This 18th-century invention was an optical instrument which people took with them on country walks in order to look at Nature. It produced a muzzy, idealised, artificially-coloured version of landscape, and influenced the painting style of the period.)

Another technical device is *antithesis*, that is the contrasting of opposites. Dividing the line into two halves encourages the display of contrasting ideas, in which noun is opposed to noun, phrase to phrase, etc. Even the grammar of one half can be made to echo or contrast with the other. The abuse of antitheses provoked Keats to refer to the heroic couplet as a rocking-horse. Even in Pope one can see the poet *forcing* his material into antitheses, fabricating contrasts in the verse which have no real existence in the matter being communicated. (In a similar way Oscar Wilde forced all his characters to speak in epigrams, just as G. K. Chesterton compelled his thoughts to take the form of paradoxes.)

The antithesis, which simplifies life by expressing it in terms of two opposing forces, Dryden found congenial, for his basic outlook did exactly this. The clean-cut clarity of the device also lends statements an air of finality—very useful for satire or argument. Here are but a few examples of his use of this device, all taken from *Absalom and Achitophel*, a poem which bases itself on the antithesis of good and evil:

> But life can never be sincerely blessed;
> Heaven punishes the bad and proves the best.

The contrast in ideas may be expressed in two contrasting lines:

> Youth, beauty, graceful action seldom fail:
> But common interest always will prevail . . .

Or the contrast can be developed within one line:

54

In midst of health imagine a disease . . .

The most may err as grossly as the few . . .

No king could govern nor no God could please . . .

I shall leave it to the computer to say how many antithetical lines there are in this poem. Apart from the celebrated portraits, which exploit the antithetical traits in their subjects (and practically every character from Charles to Shaftesbury is a bundle of conflicting traits), there are many passages of argument which proceed by way of repeated antitheses:

> . . . distinguish friends from foes;
> And try their strength, before they came to blows.
> Yet all was coloured with a smooth pretence
> Of spacious love, and duty to their prince.
> Religion, and redress of grievances,
> Two names, that always cheat and always please,
> Are often urged; and good king David's life
> Endangered by a brother and a wife.
> Thus, in a pageant show, a plot is made;
> And peace itself is war in masquerade.

And so our study of some aspects of Dryden's technique suggests that also at the level of verbal devices we can detect a relationship between form and matter, between, for example, the use of antitheses and the general tendency of Dryden to view life as a contest between contrasting forces. The idea of good *v.* evil, in *Absalom and Achitophel*, is mirrored in the couplet's devices of contrast. The battle between spirit and matter reveals itself throughout his poems in the contrast between an abstract vocabulary of ideas and the heavy, concrete images which express the appetites, the life of the flesh. The physical impact of this imagery is remarkable, and gives to Dryden's poetry its characteristic quality of earthy gusto. Sometimes the physical world is nauseating—the 'thick skull', the 'monstrous mass of foul corrupted matter', the 'steaming ordures', or the 'gouty hands'—but Dryden also relished the world of matter. His heaven is a 'bank above', or is filled with real choirs (Anne Killigrew being amongst them), and God himself is seen to 'nod' approval to Charles II's speech. The Almighty also seizes a fire-extinguisher (for quenching candles) and 'hoods the flames' of the Fire of London. Throwing mud at Shadwell or various Fanatics is made to seem like an invigorating game. For all his intellectual bent—perhaps as an antidote to it—Dryden's verse is often most attractive when he crams it joyously with physical details. These two aspects of his work—the intellectual and the physical—will be seen in the poems which we shall now examine in appropriate groups (rather than in chronological order), but as I can merely suggest that we should not neglect his numerous translations, I would like to give a taste of them by quoting the opening of Juvenal's Sixth Satire, with its superb fusing of ideas and physical verbal gusto:

> In Saturn's reign, at Nature's early birth,
> There was that thing called chastity on earth;
> When in a narrow cave, their common shade,
> The sheep, the shepherds, and their gods were laid:
> When reeds and leaves, and hides of beasts were spread
> By mountain housewives for their homely bed,
> And mossy pillows raised, for the rude husband's head.
> Unlike the niceness of our modern dames,
> (Affected nymphs with new affected names:)
> The Cynthias and the Lesbias of our years,
> Who for a sparrow's death dissolve in tears.
> Those first unpolished matrons, big and bold,
> Gave suck to infants of gigantic mould;
> Rough as their savage lords who ranged the wood,
> And fat with acorns belched their windy food.

The Poems

5

Songs and Music Odes

The modern pop-song, when performed by a writhing, metallic-costumed singer to a backing of electronic musical gimmicks, has an incredible mass-appeal. If you manage to distinguish the words, you will find they are usually ultra-simple and repetitive, with the theme ranging between romantic and erotic. The verbal element, in fact, is almost negligible (and in scat-singing becomes mere nonsense syllables or grunts). There have been periods in which the words of a song have been as important as the setting —one thinks of medieval ballads or Elizabethan lyrics—and the songs of outstanding writers such as Shakespeare, Jonson or Burns can be appreciated as poems without their accompanying music. Few of Dryden's poems can stand this isolation from their performance, usually by an actress with all the additional glamour of a stage production. Most of the settings have survived, and the short opera *King Arthur*, with music by Purcell, the greatest composer of the period, is available on a record. Dryden's songs were written for performance, and it is not really fair to judge them in cold print, which reveals their frequent insipidity and shallow conventionality.

As one might expect of songs written for the Restoration stage, erotic themes predominate, with romantic or cynical overtones as required by the particular play. The frankly sexual songs are in fact Dryden's best, having an insolent vitality and a strong rhythmic pulse, whereas the dreamy, sad or pastoral romantic lyrics are too often commonplace in ideas and idiom. Two pieces from *An Evening's Love* illustrate Dryden's talent in the saucy vein. The first one might be called comic-erotic. Here is the opening stanza:

> Calm was the even and clear was the sky,
> And the new budding flowers did spring,
> When all alone went Amyntas and I
> To hear the sweet nightingale sing;
> I sat, and he laid him down by me;
> But scarcely his breath he could draw;
> For when with a fear he began to draw near,
> He was dashed with a ha ha ha ha!

The emphatic rhythm makes us want to sing this cheerful, cheeky song, and the amusing, dactyllic lilt (a happy feature of some fifteen songs) is heard again in the next one, with its sensual details and the curious erotic idiom ('accords me the blessing'):

> After the pangs of a desperate lover,
> When day and night I have sighed all in vain,
> Ah what a pleasure it is to discover
> In her eyes pity, who causes my pain! . . .
>
> When the denial comes fainter and fainter,
> And her eyes give what her tongue does deny,
> Ah what a trembling I feel when I venture,
> Ah what a trembling does usher my joy!
>
> When, with a sigh, she accords me the blessing,
> And her eyes twinkle 'twixt pleasure and pain;
> Ah what a joy 'tis beyond all expressing,
> Ah what a joy to hear, 'Shall we again?'

'Doin' what comes natcherly' sings the brazen heroine of *Annie Get Your Gun* to matinée audiences of aunties and children. John Dryden seems almost refined by comparison! He did become nearly as dully instructive as the modern sex-manual in a song from *Marriage à la Mode*, but employed the current erotic slang ('die', 'breathe his last' and similar terms) and the banal love idiom of the day, neatly enough:

> Whilst Alexis lay pressed
> In her arms he loved best,

With his hands round her neck
And his head on her breast,
He found the fierce pleasure too hasty to stay,
And his soul in the tempest just flying away . . .

The youth, though in haste,
And breathing his last,
In pity died slowly, while she died more fast;
Till at length she cried, 'Now, my dear, now let us go,
Now die, my Alexis, and I will die too.'

Thus entranced they did lie,
Till Alexis did try
To recover new breath, that again he might die:
Then often they died; but the more they did so,
The nymph died more quick, and the shepherd more slow.

I think an age which can freely buy lurid novels on a railway
bookstall will hardly blush at these quaintly genteel attempts at
being daring, though no doubt the pretty Nell Gwynns or Anne
Bracegirdles made the most of the innuendos as they sang them
on the stage.

A song that appeared in the collection *Sylvae* as late as 1685 is
attributed to Dryden, and was even translated later into Latin. It
is another example of the comic-erotic, and displays Dryden's
liking for rather obvious rhythmic effects—which are possibly
suited to setting to music. The second stanza injects an unusual
political note into the amusing anecdote:

Sylvia the fair, in the bloom of fifteen,
Felt an innocent warmth, as she lay on the green;
She had heard of a pleasure, and something she guessed
By the tousing and tumbling and touching her breast;
She saw the men eager, but was at a loss,
What they meant by their sighing, and kissing so close;
    By their praying and whining
    And clasping and twining,
    And panting and wishing,
    And sighing and kissing
    And sighing and kissing so close.

'Ah,' she cried, 'ah for a languishing maid
In a country of Christians to die without aid!
Not a Whig, or a Tory, or Trimmer at least,
Or a Protestant parson, or Catholic priest,
To instruct a young virgin, that is at a loss
What they meant by their sighing, and kissing so close! . . .'

I am not sure whether the *Song for a Girl* (from *Love Triumphant*)
is cynical or ironical, but it has some of Dryden's clear-eyed
realism which is more acceptable than his banal romantic efforts:

Young I am, and yet unskilled
How to make a lover yield:
How to keep, or how to gain;
When to love, and when to feign:

Take me, take me, some of you,
While I yet am young and true,
Ere I can my soul disguise,
Heave my breasts, and roll my eyes.

Stay not till I learn the way,
How to lie, and to betray:
He that has me first, is blessed,
For I may deceive the rest.

Could I find a blooming youth;
Full of love, and full of truth,
Brisk, and of a jaunty mien,
I should long to be fifteen.

She is partly insolent, partly disillusioned, and this mood is found
often in Dryden's comedies, perhaps reflecting something real in
him and the more sensitive members of his audience.

The romantic-erotic song (which is still with us) also occurs in
many of Dryden's plays, but the words are scarcely memorable.
The Conquest of Granada tells of the lover's sensual dreams:

Beneath a myrtle shade
Which Love for none but happy lovers made,
I slept, and straight my Love before me brought
Phyllis the object of my waking thought;

Undressed she came my flames to meet,
While Love strewed flowers beneath her feet;
Flowers, which so pressed by her, became more sweet.

The eroticism gets rather smothered in the stale idiom in so many of these songs. 'Melting kisses/Murmuring Blisses', sighs Amynta. ''Tis a pleasure, a pleasure to sigh and to languish', sing two anonymous lovers. 'Now cold as ice I am, now hot as fire,/I dare not tell myself my own desire', sings coy Phyllis in *The Assignation*. Nor is the 'pastoral dialogue' of Thyrsis and Iris any more remarkable verbally: 'He said, O kiss me longer,/And longer yet and longer,/If you will make me blessed.'

The purely romantic songs are even more naïvely swoony, and the typical jigging rhythms Dryden employs often give an effect of parody:

Wherever I am, and whatever I do;
My Phyllis is still in my mind:
When angry I mean not to Phyllis to go,
My feet of themselves the way find . . .

And where the lines have an interesting lilt there is the disappointment of a threadbare idiom, as we see in the song from *Secret Love*:

I feed a flame within which so torments me
That it both pains my heart, and yet contents me:
'Tis such a pleasing smart, and I so love it,
That I had rather die, than once remove it.

So it is rather a relief to return to the vigour of the cynical lyrics, one of which neatly and frankly asks:

Why should a foolish marriage vow
Which long ago was made,
Oblige us to each other now
When passion is decayed?

And there is something disarmingly candid about Mercury's song to Phaedra:

Fair Iris I love, and hourly I die,
But not for a lip, nor a languishing eye:

61

She's fickle and false, and there we agree;
For I am as false, and as fickle as she:
We neither believe what either can say;
And, neither believing, we neither betray.

From this it is rather a far cry to the jolly debunking in the rustic song from the opera *King Arthur*, delightfully set to music by Purcell:

We ha' cheated the parson, we'll cheat him again;
For why should a blockhead ha' One in Ten? . . .
For prating so long like a book-learn'd sot,
Till pudding and dumpling burn to pot . . .
We'll toss off our ale till we canno' stand,
And Hoigh for the Honour of Old England. . . .

One can already hear in this the innocent joviality of Goldsmith's *She Stoops to Conquer*—still alive in Tennyson's unintentionally hilarious melodrama *The Promise of May*. But Dryden did not often exploit this vein. Indeed there are quite a few non-erotic songs, varied in theme and idiom, which suggest that given the occasion Dryden might have written in a more original manner than he did. *The Epithalamium* in the play *Amboyna* throws a somewhat brutal light on contemporary marriage customs:

The bridegroom comes, he comes apace
With love and fury in his face;
She shrinks away, he close pursues,
And prayers and threats, at once does use . . .

That bitter comedy *The Kind Keeper* has an equally bitter song, in an idiom far from romantic:

'Gainst keepers we petition,
Who would enclose the common:
'Tis enough to raise sedition
In the free-born subject woman.
Because for his gold
I my body have sold,
He thinks I'm a slave for my life;
He rants, domineers,
He swaggers and swears,
And would keep me as bare as his wife.

'Round thy coasts, fair nymph of Britain' (in *King Arthur*) offers patriotic praise of British fish, sheep and coal-mines. *Love Triumphant* includes a rather spasmodic attack on 'O jealousy!/ 'Tis all from thee,/O jealousy!/Thou tyrant, tyrant jealousy,/ Thou tyrant of the mind!' and *The Lady's Song*, published in *Poetical Miscellanies*, 1704, although pastoral in flavour, actually refers to the banished King James and his beautiful consort Mary, and offers seditious advice to armed rebellion:

> While Pan, and fair Syrinx, are fled from our shore,
> The Graces are banished, and love is no more . . .
> But if you dare think of deserving our charms,
> Away with your sheephooks, and take to your arms . . .

Finally, among these rather more original compositions, we must place the only hymn with certainty ascribed to Dryden—the translation of the *Veni Creator Spiritus*. Sacred songs are notoriously prone to heavy clichés, clumsy rhetoric or maudlin sentiments. ('Jesus wants me for a sunbeam', or 'Here I raise my Ebenezer' are random examples of hymns that now embarrass.) Dryden's paraphrase is cluttered with musty imagery: 'Thrice holy fount, thrice holy fire,/Our hearts with heavenly love inspire . . .' but one stanza breathes something of his typical energy:

> Refine and purge our earthy parts;
> But, oh, inflame and fire our hearts!
> Our frailties help, our vice control;
> Submit the senses to the soul;
> And when rebellious they are grown,
> Then, lay thy hand, and hold 'em down.

Dryden, we see, expands the laconic '*fons vivus*' to 'thrice holy fount', which is empty rhetoric, but the stanza quoted above improves upon the rather abstract original—'*Infirma nostri corporis virtute firmans perpeti*'.

Obviously a song-writer must consider the technical problems of what words and rhythms are best suited to a musical setting. Dryden did in fact comment on this, but it is clear from many songs, with their strong beats and repeated phrases, that he tried to meet the composer half-way. On the page the devices seem too unsubtle, but perhaps not in the sung performance:

Hark, hark, the waters fall, fall, fall;
And with a murmuring sound
Dash, dash upon the ground . . .

Perhaps the most bizarre example is from *Tyrannic Love*, in which Nakar and Damilcar descend in clouds and sing in this manner:

Merry, merry, merry, we sail from the east.
Half tippled at a rainbow feast . . .
Tivy, tivy, tivy, we mount and we fly . . .
We slide on the back of a new-falling star.
And drop from above,
In a jelly of love! . . .
That, silent and swift, the little soft god
Is here with a wish, and is gone with a nod.

The Sea Fight (from *Amboyna*) attempts to recapture the drama of battle, and uses naval terms with gusto:

Now now they grapple, and now board amain,
Blow up the hatches, they're off all again:
Give 'em a broadside, the dice run at all,
Down comes the mast and yard, and tacklings fall,
She grows giddy now like blind fortune's wheel,
She sinks there, she sinks, she turns up her keel.
Whoever beheld so noble a sight
As this so brave, so bloody sea fight?

Another battle, in *King Arthur*, relies on simple imitation of sounds or actions:

We come, we come, we come, we come,
Says the double, double, double beat of the thundering drum . . .
They fly, they fly, they fly, they fly;
Victoria, Victoria, the bold Britons cry.

These words are hardly more than cues for the music, but they do suggest the basic devices of the celebrated music odes. On occasion, however, Dryden is able to salt these naïve tricks with a dash of eroticism, as in this curious scene of King Arthur being tempted by two Sirens who 'show themselves to the waist' and sing:

> Two daughters of this aged stream are we:
> And both our sea-green locks have combed for thee:
> Come bathe with us an hour or two,
> Come naked in, for we are so;
> What danger from a naked foe?
> Come bathe with us, come bathe and share
> What pleasures in the floods appear;
> We'll beat the waters till they bound,
> And circle round, around, around,
> And circle round, around.

We begin to see why *King Arthur* was such a success when performed. Indeed, its scores of dances and scenic miracles ('An island arises, to a soft tune' says one stage direction blandly) must have been far more striking than the smoothly banal song in it, which has remained one of Dryden's most often sung pieces:

> Fairest isle, all isles excelling,
> Seat of pleasures, and of loves:
> Venus here will choose her dwelling,
> And forsake her Cyprian groves . . .

We now turn to the celebrated music odes and the *Secular Masque*—all 'occasional' poems. Indeed the occasion for the music odes affords an interesting sidelight on London musical life. On St. Cecilia's Day, from 1683 to 1710, the patroness of music was celebrated by the Musical Society with a concert, consisting of an ode performed by a chorus of sixty voices, soloists and an orchestra of some twenty instruments. Before the concert there was divine service at St. Bride's, and after it a feast. The 1685 concert was a failure and none was given in 1686. Dryden's *A Song for St. Cecilia's Day, 1687* was commissioned in an attempt to revive the annual celebration, and it was set to music by Giovanni Baptista Draghi, though the setting heard today is the much later one by Handel. The performance was a great success. Ten years later Dryden provided his second music ode, *Alexander's Feast*, for which he was paid £40. Incidentally, the tradition of writing Cecilian odes ended with Thornton's burlesque, written in 1749, and accompanied by suitable music on the salt-box, Jew's-harp, marrowbones, cleavers and hurdy-gurdy!

The Cecilia ode, in free Pindaric style, divides into three parts. The opening stanza associates music with the divine harmony which created an ordered universe out of the 'jarring atoms' of chaos:

> From harmony, from heavenly harmony
> This universal frame began:
> From harmony to harmony
> Through all the compass of the notes it ran,
> The diapason closing full in man.

This is a witty use of musical terminology (*diapason* is the octave, the perfect consonance, and also the basic organ pipe) appropriate to the occasion, yet a serious affirmation by Dryden that the universe is divinely ordered and that music is of divine origin. (Elsewhere Dryden makes similar high claims for poetry and painting.)

The middle section begins by exclaiming 'What passion cannot music raise and quell!' and gives the example of Jubal playing the 'corded shell' (the tortoise-shell, stringed to produce the first lyre). Five strophes demonstrate the special qualities of trumpet, drum, flute, lute, violin and organ. The rather crude attempts at imitating sounds, which we have noted in the songs, are here transformed into subtle evocations of instrumental tone-colours by ingenious rhythmic and consonantal effects:

> The trumpet's loud clangour
> Excites us to arms
> With shrill notes of anger
> And mortal alarms . . .

> Sharp violins proclaim
> Their jealous pangs, and desperation,
> Fury, frantic indignation,
> Depth of pains, and height of passion . . .

This is not profound poetry, but perfect craftsmanship.

According to legend, the saint's prayers summoned an angel to her on her wedding-night to convince her pagan husband she was intended for God's service. Dryden makes the angel appear at the wonderful sound of the organ. Perhaps Dryden's contemporaries liked the witty adaptations of incidents. Everybody knew that St. Cecilia's prayers summoned an angel so why not transform the miracle a little by connecting it with the 'sacred organ', whose notes fly to heaven and improve the celestial choirs?

The final 'grand chorus' returns to the idea of the harmonious universe which, at the sound of Gabriel's trumpet, will be 'untuned', destroyed by the same harmonious power that created it. The lines are sombre, and remind us of Dryden's deep feelings about the end of the world (which can be seen again in the Killigrew ode):

> So when the last and dreadful hour
> This crumbling pageant shall devour,
> The trumpet shall be heard on high,
> The dead shall live, the living die,
> And music shall untune the sky.

Poets are often at the mercy of composers, and it would be interesting to hear the original setting which stretched these laconic lines to 'And music shall untune the sky, untune, untune, and music shall, and music shall, and music shall untune, and music shall untune the sky'. In his second Cecilian ode Dryden made sure there were plenty of repeated phrases for the composer to juggle with. The first chorus celebrates the warrior-emperor Alexander and Thais the courtesan with simple gusto:

> Happy, happy, happy pair!
> None but the brave
> None but the brave
> None but the brave deserves the fair.

The sub-title of the ode is 'the power of music', and to illustrate the ancient notion that music had a direct effect on the listener's mood, Dryden took the well-known story of the musician Timotheus, at a banquet, moving the emperor to anger and tears by his varied playing. Perhaps Dryden had read Jeremy Collier's account of this scene, published the same year as his ode:

'One time, when Alexander was at dinner, this man played him a Phrygian air: the prince immediately rises, snatches up his lance, and puts himself in a posture of fighting. And the retreat was no sooner sounded by the change of the harmony, but his arms were grounded, and his fire extinct, and he sat down as orderly as if he had come from one of Aristotle's lectures.' One cannot help finding this scene comic, as though Alexander were a puppet, jerked into one mood after another at the command of the musician. Dryden, of course, offers an even more startling series of rapid transformations—Alexander thinks he's a god, fights his battles over again, weeps at the fate of Darius, melts with love on the breast of his mistress, is suddenly filled with the rage for vengeance and sets fire to his palace! The quick-change artist of this breathless melodrama is something less than 'the god-like hero' to whom we are introduced in the first strophe. His behaviour is a little too like the antics of a stage hypnotist's victim to command our respect for him or for the power of the music. In fact, it makes us call in question the contemporary myth that music could have such a direct and all-controlling effect on a human being, and so the ode becomes a glorious bit of musical hullabaloo. As van Doren suggests, thinking no doubt of the brassy choruses, it 'perhaps is only immortal ragtime'.

But if we do not take it too seriously, surely we can all enjoy immortal ragtime. In fact some passages are immortal opera. Here is the scene evoking the legend of Alexander's divine origins, his mother Olympia having been ravished by Jove, disguised, as was his wont on these frequent adventures, as a dragon:

A dragon's fiery form belied the god:
Sublime on radiant spires he rode,
When he to fair Olympia pressed:
And while he sought her snowy breast:
Then, round her slender waist he curled,
And stamped an image of himself, a sovereign of the world.

Jolly Bacchus, the god of wine, is even more fun, and the appropriately noisy trumpets and drums set the mood for the heady, tipsy chorus:

Bacchus' blessings are a treasure;
Drinking is the soldier's pleasure;
Rich the treasure;
Sweet the pleasure;
Sweet is pleasure after pain.

Dryden adds a happy touch of humour when he tells how the king, inspired by the music (and the wine?):

Fought all his battles o'er again;
And thrice he routed all his foes; and thrice he slew the slain.

But pity seizes him as he hears of Darius:

Fallen, fallen, fallen, fallen,
Fallen from his high estate . . .

and pity then merges with love as the music directs him to abandon the 'toil and trouble' of war and turn to the 'lovely Thais' at his side:

The prince, unable to conceal his pain,
Gazed on the fair
Who caused his care,
And sighed and looked, sighed and looked,
Sighed and looked, and sighed again:
At length, with love and wine at once oppressed,
The vanquished victor sunk upon her breast.

One cannot help feeling that a certain maudlin inebriation has overcome the monarch. At this moment is he really any different from a score of sentimental Restoration gallants who have drunk a glass too many?

Asleep though he now is, Alexander is to be roused again by the golden lyre of Timotheus, and inspired by the music and the ghastly band of snake-like hissing Furies, he seizes a torch and follows Thais to set ablaze the palace. Only at this point does Dryden make the customary reference to St. Cecilia, and comparing her summoning of an angel and Timotheus' musical power of persuading Alexander that he was a god, he ends with a neat piece of wit:

Let old Timotheus yield the prize,
Or both divide the crown;
He raised a mortal to the skies;
She drew an angel down.

A vicious conclusion, thundered Dr. Johnson, because the angel really descended, whereas Alexander was only metaphorically deified. True enough, but in their way both the power of prayer and the power of music can work miracles. The ode is, of course, a celebration of music, a verbal parallel to the changing musical modes which it portrays. But if we take the poem too seriously we must conclude that the legend essentially denigrates both Alexander and the nature of music, reducing him to a puppet and the 'heavenly harmony' to a hypnotic trick. But as a rococo entertainment *Alexander's Feast*, the setting of which is lost, is delightful enough, although to me it remains superficial when compared with the first ode for St. Cecilia.

Dryden died on 1 May 1700, it being, according to tradition, the third night of the performance of his *Secular Masque*, a short piece included in a revival of Fletcher's *The Pilgrim*, and set to music by Daniel Purcell and others. It was the turn of the century (as *secular*, from the Latin *saeculum*, implies) and a good occasion for the three gods, Janus, Chronos and Momus, to review the age. Chronos (*Time*) enters with a scythe in his hand and a great globe on his back. His speech might easily be that of the aged poet, ready at last to say farewell to the weight of worldly cares:

Weary, weary of my weight,
Let me, let me drop my freight,
And leave the world behind.
I could not bear
Another year
The load of human-kind.

Diana, the huntress, enters to the sound of horns, representing presumably the court of James I:

With horns and with hounds I waken the day,
And hie to my woodland walks away;

I tuck up my robe, and am buskined soon,
And tie to my forehead a waxing moon.
I course the fleet stag, unkennel the fox,
And chase the wild goats o'er summits of rocks,
With shouting and hooting we pierce through the sky,
And Echo turns hunter, and doubles the cry.

The gods agree that it was a golden age, gay and carefree, and
none too serious—the verse itself mirrors the mood:

Then our age was in its prime,
Free from rage, and free from crime,
A very merry, dancing, drinking,
Laughing, quaffing, and unthinking time.

After a dance by Diana's attendants, Mars, the god of war,
representing the civil wars of Charles I's reign, enters proclaim-
ing 'arms and honour' and dismisses lazy peace (together with
plenty and pleasure, however). Momus indeed reprimands the
warrior god with these disillusioned words:

Thy sword within the scabbard keep,
And let mankind agree;
Better the world were fast asleep,
Than kept awake by thee.
The fools are only thinner,
With all our cost and care;
But neither side a winner,
For things are as they were.

Is this bitterness or wisdom? Does Dryden, in 1700, see the nation
still as divided as it was in 1642?

Venus appears, the appropriate goddess for the amorous
worlds of Charles II and James II, we assume. 'Joy ruled the day,
and love the night,' Chronos exclaims, adding what is perhaps a
hidden reference to the exiled queen of James:

But since the queen of pleasure left the ground,
I faint, I lag,
And feebly drag
The ponderous orb around.

The masque ends with a marvellously laconic chorus, as Momus points to Diana, Mars and Venus in turn, with appropriate accusations:

All, all, of a piece throughout;
Thy chase had a beast in view;
Thy wars brought nothing about;
Thy lovers were all untrue.
'Tis well an old age is out,
And time to begin a new.

Merely a few lines in a brief, unspectacular masque, but the stark phrases strike home with deadly effect as the whole century is dismissed as tainted, unproductive, faithless. One thinks of the naked, bitter style of the older Yeats and realises that the versatile poet of saucy songs and dazzling odes had also this talent, rarely seen, for bare, poignant, clear-sighted 'poetry of statement'. Each line *is* a direct statement, but so distilled and controlled that it is raised to memorable and moving poetry.

Anne Killigrew painted by herself.

Brouncker, Charles II and Bacon.

The Sea Triumph of Charles II by Antonio Verrio.

The Presentation of a Pineapple to Charles II.

6

Elegies

Today the word *elegy* has an old-fashioned ring, signifying something too formal and conventional for our casual, unbuttoned age. Yet the deaths of Dylan Thomas, President Kennedy and Pope John, to mention but a few, inspired poets to public utterance. At moments of intense feeling men turn to poetry to express their grief. Too frequently the result is the pathetic doggerel of the newspaper deaths-column, or the slick journalism of the professional obituary. We remember Milton's dignified lament:

> For Lycidas is dead, dead ere his prime,
> Young Lycidas, and hath not left his peer . . .

or Shelley's exalted song upon Keats:

> Whilst, burning through the inmost veil of heaven,
> The soul of Adonais, like a star,
> Beacons from the abode where the Eternal are.

But we forget the countless insipid elegies, the loyal odes on dead monarchs (sometimes in the 17th century printed between alternate black pages) or the sincere but ludicrous versifying of amateur poets, of which this one on the death of King Edward VII is an amusing example:

> The will of God we must obey.
> Dreadful—our king taken away! . . .
> His mighty work for the nation,
> Making peace and strengthening union—
> Always at it since on the throne—
> Saved the country more than one billion.

I think this is worth quoting to indicate some of the hazards of public lamentation. Dryden must have known that the official celebration of births, marriages and deaths, often for a considerable fee, would inevitably lead to feats of flattery and ingenuity on the part of poets anxious to please an audience which appreciated verbal fireworks. Moreover, it was the custom to print elegies by several hands in a sort of souvenir edition, and naturally this would encourage poets to vie with each other in producing something spectacular. (Dryden's elegy on Hastings was printed in such an edition, side by side with poems by Herrick, Denham and Marvell.) Eventually the elegy became such a stale convention that Dr. Johnson could only sigh with weariness, while parodies of the convention came from Gray, with his *Ode on the Death of a Favourite Cat Drowned in a Tub of Goldfishes*, or from Cowper with his *On the Death of Mrs. Throckmorton's Bulfinch* and similar mock elegies.

Dryden accepted the conditions imposed by his times, but he managed to manipulate flattery and technical tricks for deeper purposes. Obviously he earned his fees and pleased his patrons: his poems served an immediate function. But as we shall see, as we examine his elegies, these 'occasional' poems often rise above the events which inspired them and become lasting works of art. Just as journalism sometimes becomes literature, so does the conventional elegy evolve, in Dryden's hands, in a most varied and imaginative way. Strictly speaking an elegy is a 'song of lamentation, especially for the dead', but in Dryden's poems the tone of the lament is mingled with praise, confident faith, even humour, and this is why he also calls his elegies 'heroic stanzas' or a 'funeral Pindaric' or an 'ode'. Few poets have ranged so widely within what seems a narrow genre.

Upon the Death of the Lord Hastings, published in 1649, celebrates the nineteen-year-old youth who died a victim to small-pox, on the eve of the day arranged for his marriage with the daughter of the royal physician. The bride's father no doubt appreciated Dryden's ingenious description of the medical symptoms:

> Blisters with pride swelled; which through 's flesh did sprout
> Like rose-buds, stuck i' th' lily-skin about.

Each little pimple had a tear in it,
To wail the fault its rising did commit . . .

We may feel that this wit is misplaced, but the bereaved parents
and friends probably did not. Verbal ingenuity was the poetic
fashion, and was appreciated even on tombstones. Dryden, himself only eighteen, is merely following Cowley, Cleveland and
other imitators of Donne. The young poet obviously wishes to
display his classical learning, but he also includes up-to-date
allusions to the celebrated Danish astronomer Tycho Brahe, and
to the execution of Charles I earlier in the year, which he con-
demns as 'the nation's sin'. What is most striking is that the witty
style ruins Dryden's characteristic talent for clarity. The effort to
construct paradoxes results in lines of jerky, tortuous expression:

Is death (sin's wages) grace's now? Shall art
Make us more learned, only to depart?
If merit be disease, if virtue death;
To be good, not to be; who'd then bequeath
Himself to discipline? Who'd not esteem
Labour a crime, study self-murder deem?

The stumbling rhythms and clumsy phrases of this early poem
are obvious enough, but it is more important to note Dryden's
serious religious and political concern. He does question himself
about the seeming futility of a virtuous life which can suddenly
be ended by disease. Moreover he is already developing his
typical method of starting with a private event and expanding it,
by comparisons and argument, to include larger public events. In
this poem the traitorous malady is spoken of in terms of the
recent civil war and the beheading of the king. The proud
blisters of the smallpox,

. . . rebel-like, with their own lord at strife,
Thus made an insurrection 'gainst his life.

The penitential tears of the pustules inspire some ludicrous
phrases, but Dryden implies that England will likewise have to
repent and weep for its political sin. So already we see how a

poem on a limited subject can grow into something of greater import.

Ten years later the *Heroic Stanzas* commemorate the death of the man largely responsible for the king's execution. Here, in solemn four-line stanzas, Oliver Cromwell is praised for his God-given virtues, his military skill, his peaceful aims. The quatrains are stiff and formal, like the slow march of soldiers at a state funeral. A saintly but active man seems to have been sent by heaven to cleanse and fortify the nation. Dryden's sense of awe, of human dignity, responds to the death of a towering historical figure, but of personal grief there is little evidence:

> His grandeur he derived from heaven alone,
> For he was great ere fortune made him so;
> And wars like mists that rise against the sun
> Made him but greater seem, not greater grow . . .
>
> Swift and resistless through the land he passed
> Like that bold Greek who did the east subdue;
> And made to battles such heroic haste
> As if on wings of victory he flew . . .
>
> His ashes in a peaceful urn shall rest,
> His name a great example stands to show
> How strangely high endeavours may be blessed,
> Where piety and valour jointly go.

In 1685 the fifty-four-year-old Poet Laureate writes an official lament, *Threnodia Augustalis*, for Charles II, using the flexible lyrical form of the Pindaric ode. The sudden and painful last illness of the king, who 'went through the agonies of death with a calm and a constancy, that amazed all who were about him', as Burnet recorded, is painted with emphatic strokes by Dryden. The declamatory manner and the harsh details (the dead king is called a 'senseless lump of sacred clay') are perhaps hard for a modern reader to accept. Here is the scene when the Duke of York visits the chamber of death:

> Arrived within the mournful room, he saw
> A wild distraction, void of awe,
> And arbitrary grief unbounded by a law.

God's image, God's anointed lay
Without motion, pulse or breath,
A senseless lump of sacred clay,
An image, now, of death.
Amidst his sad attendants' groans and cries,
The lines of that adored, forgiving face,
Distorted from their native grace;
An iron slumber sat on his majestic eyes.

When Dryden praises a man he is never half-hearted about it. The Duke is Charles's 'pious brother, sure the best/Who ever bore that name', and Charles's courage and sufferings, real though they were, are magnified:

In five such days he suffered more
Than any suffered in his reign before . . .

Dryden does not hesitate to compare him with God, for Charles is

That all-forgiving king,
The type of Him above,
That inexhausted spring
Of clemency and love . . .

This is an appropriate occasion for Dryden to take stock of the Restoration, and again he offers us undiluted praise:

For all those joys thy restoration brought,
For all the miracles it wrought,
For all the healing barm thy mercy poured
Into the nation's bleeding wound,
And care that after kept it sound,
For numerous blessings yearly showered,
And property with plenty crowned;
For freedom, still maintained alive,
Freedom which in no other land will thrive,
Freedom an English subject's sole prerogative,
Without whose charms even peace would be
But a dull quiet slavery . . .

Not unnaturally, after itemising Charles's virtues ('Forgiving, bounteous, humble, just and kind') and assuring us that our former royal 'patron' is now 'our guardian angel', Dryden looks to the future and ends on a note of optimistic, not to say jingoistic, patriotism. He has a vision of

> The long retinue of a prosperous reign,
> A series of successful years,
> In orderly array, a martial, manly train.
> Behold even to remoter shores
> A conquering navy proudly spread;
> The British cannon formidably roars . . .

Modern readers, deafened from all sides by competing propaganda media, are not likely to swallow Dryden's lavish praise, loud declamations and exaggerated grief or joy without grimacing or, perhaps, smiling cynically. Even those who are attracted to the Merry Monarch hardly see him as the 'type of Him above', and few historians would view the Duke of York as 'a monarch ripened for a throne'—at all events he only managed to keep it for a bare three years. This is not to deny Dryden's skill. There is always his characteristic vigour, the confident ringing line, or the striking phrase:

> So much thy foes thy manly mind mistook,
> Who judged it by the mildness of thy look:
> Like a well-tempered sword, it bent at will;
> But kept the native toughness of the steel.

Perhaps the best way to appreciate such a poem now is in the way we enjoy Italian opera. We applaud the frenzied aria, the gaudy emotionalism, the grandiose orchestration, but we do not take the melodramatic characters and plot too seriously. Dryden did not *mean* us to accept his poem as a piece of technical virtuosity, but we can hardly praise or lament Charles II on Dryden's terms today. Many indeed would be more impressed by a different style, by, for instance, the dignified underplaying of Marvell's lines on the execution of Charles's father:

> He nothing common did or mean
> Upon that memorable scene:
>   But with his keener eye
>   The axe's edge did try:

Nor called the gods with vulgar spite
To vindicate his helpless right,
  But bowed his comely head,
  Down as upon a bed.

In the previous year, 1684, Dryden published his well-known lines *To the Memory of Mr. Oldham*. John Oldham, twenty-two years younger than Dryden, had died in 1683 at the age of thirty, but his *Satires upon the Jesuits*, written in 1679, brought him fame. Dryden probably only knew him from 1681, but presumably was encouraged by Oldham's example when he turned to satire himself. Dryden openly declared himself a Roman Catholic in 1685, so it is ironical to find him praising as his twin-soul the author of highly scurrilous anti-Catholic verses —the recent Muses Library edition is still an expurgated one. This passage will give some idea of Oldham's attitudes and the 'rugged line' which Dryden very delicately criticised in his elegy:

Or let that wholesome statute be revived,
Which England heretofore from wolves relieved;
Tax every shire instead of them to bring
Each year a certain tale of Jesuits in;
And let their mangled quarters hang the isle
To scare all future vermin from the soil.
Monsters avaunt! may some kind whirlwind sweep
Our land, and drown these locusts in the deep . . .

Of Dryden's farewell to Oldham, T. S. Eliot has remarked: 'From the perfection of such an elegy we cannot detract . . .' and Mark van Doren says: 'If one is not pleased by the lines . . . one will not be pleased by anything in Dryden', adding, 'There is not an original word in the work. It is a classical mosaic . . .' What Dryden has captured is the dignified, formal style of the classical elegy; when read aloud the poem impresses with its bell-like tolling rhymes, its easy unfolding of ideas, its solemn rhetoric:

Once more, hail and farewell; farewell thou young,
But ah too short, Marcellus of our tongue;
Thy brows with ivy, and with laurels bound;
But fate and gloomy night encompass thee around.

79

With this are mingled the personal touches ('Whom I began to think and call my own') in which the notion of fellow-poets and friendly rivals is stressed. Throughout the poem the simple but appropriate image of *fruition* is varied by reference to Oldham's talent being 'early ripe' and therefore, in his satires, quick (or sharp), in contrast to the mature but mellow, oversweet rhymes of older poets. It is a triumph of pastiche, of classical imitation, so that the celebration of a particular poet is also a reminder of the immense poetic tradition behind his work. It is another example of Dryden's method of developing an 'occasional' poem into something much wider.

Of course, a 'classical mosaic', however finely chosen and cemented together, cannot have the effect of newly-minted expressions, and some readers would prefer a poem with original words and ideas rather than a rehandling of traditional attitudes and vocabulary. Both types of poems make their appeals to the sensitive reader: Dryden's classically-educated contemporaries were particularly attracted to remodelled classical poems, full of allusions to Virgil or Horace or Ovid. So we might ask at this point what a classical allusion is supposed to do.

One thing it did for Dryden's reader was to recall for him those Latin or Greek texts he had studied at grammar school and university, thus establishing between writer and reader a common ground of literary experience. It would be rather like two old friends remembering together events in their past—a little nostalgic perhaps. The allusion is also an economical way of referring to quite complex matters, just as the word 'Napoleonic' can conjure up for us a whole range of historical events and ideas. The difficulty with allusions is that 'Napoleonic', for example, may for the author suggest the fiery ambition of an admired patriot, whereas the reader may think instead of a Europe torn by war and fear under the impact of a power-drunk fanatic. Somehow the author has to control the effect of his allusion so that it works in the way he wishes. I wonder whether Dryden, in the Oldham ode, has not gone so far in controlling the allusion that he almost has to rewrite Virgil. In talking of his and Oldham's friendly rivalry he says:

To the same goal did both our studies drive,
The last set out the soonest did arrive.
Thus Nisus fell upon the slippery place,
While his young friend performed and won the race.

If Dryden's reader remembers the passage in the *Aeneid* (which Dryden had just been translating) he will recall that the devoted friends, Nisus and Euryalus, were competing with others in a race. Near the finish, Nisus, by ill-luck, slipped on the grass soaked with blood of sacrificed bullocks. Dryden's translation runs:

But treading where the treacherous puddle lay,
His heels flew up; and on the grassy floor,
He fell, besmeared with filth, and holy gore.

The accident is a little comic! However, Nisus demonstrates his great friendship for Euryalus by unsportingly grabbing Salius' foot, making him also fall flat in the blood-soaked mud, and thus Euryalus is able to win the race.

We notice how Dryden has had to alter his original. Because Oldham, being younger, 'last set out', the contest now becomes a handicap race. The whole point of the Virgilian episode is that though he could not win himself, Nisus was selfless enough to help his friend to win—by his unsporting trick against Salius. Nothing of this survives in the Dryden-Oldham situation: Oldham merely wins because Dryden slips down. Now Alan Roper, in *Dryden's Poetic Kingdoms*, argues that Dryden has carefully 'edited' his allusion so that it does become relevant to the contest between Dryden and Oldham. This may be so, but one asks what is the point of referring the reader to an episode in Virgil, only to alter the details substantially so that it fits the new situation? It seems peculiar to ask the reader to *recall imperfectly* an episode in a classical poem. In a similar way one could 'edit' a biblical allusion and write: 'Thus Adam ate the orange and then gave it to his sister Eve.' One can only assume that Dryden wanted to use a classical comparison but could not find one that really fitted. I have examined this example in detail because we so easily accept the 'classical allusion' as a rapid device: Dryden's slipshod use of one here seems to me merely to confuse the picture he wishes to give us of the relationship between the two competing poets.

Nor am I sure whether Dryden's apology for Oldham's 'harsh cadence' is much more than a glib quibble:

> What could advancing age have added more?
> It might (what nature never gives the young)
> Have taught the numbers of thy native tongue.
> But satire needs not those, and wit will shine
> Through the harsh cadence of a rugged line.
> A noble error, and but seldom made,
> When poets are by too much force betrayed.
> Thy generous fruits, though gathered ere their prime
> Still showed a quickness; and maturing time
> But mellows what we write to the dull sweets of rhyme.

If satire does not need correct verse—verse which is neither harsh nor rugged—why then is such verse an 'error'? Or, if Oldham's youthful but untaught verses have been betrayed by too much force into error, why should more mature and correct verse be denigrated as 'dull sweets'? Dryden obviously thinks Oldham's verse was too rough: on the other hand he wants to praise him. So he is led to excuse him by saying that satire can be pretty rough—well, it's a good fault—and anyway the more polished rhyming is a bit dull and sugary. In his anxiety to praise, Dryden's logic is standing upon its head.

Perhaps I am being over-critical of a poem which certainly has wide appeal, and of course, I do admire its clarity, its rhythms, and its sound. But I find it a flawed masterpiece.

If the lines on Oldham have been widely praised, *Eleonora* (1692), a long poem on the Countess of Abington, has been equally widely condemned. Dryden had never met the Countess and he received a large fee for his 'panegyrical poem', as he called it. Donne in similar circumstances had composed his great *Anniversaries*, so one must not assume that a craftsman cannot write a good poem, to order, any less than architects and their artist-artisans can build a splendid cathedral. But it may well be that, as there was no personal motive for grief or praise, Dryden could justifiably make his poem into a eulogy of ideal Christian virtues. If we take the poem in this way, remembering also the contemporary fondness for wit, we shall not be surprised at the seemingly comic exaggerations with which he describes her charity, prudent management, humility, piety, or conjugal virtues—to quote but a few of the marginal glosses.

The opening lines prepare us for the technique of quaint over-statement: the Countess's death becomes public news just as rumours of the death of a king slowly filter abroad to the colonies which, in ignorance, are still in the midst of prayers for his long life. In particular, the poor learn of her death with great sorrow, because of her life-sustaining charity towards them:

> But most the poor, whom daily she supplied;
> Beginning to be such, but when she died.
> For, while she lived, they slept in peace, by night;
> Secure of bread, as of returning light;
> And, with such firm dependence on the day,
> That need grew pampered; and forgot to pray:
> So sure the dole, so ready at their call,
> They stood prepared to see the manna fall.

14-21

These, and many similar lines, could be read as mere flattery, fulsome in its excess, showing the poor dependent on the Countess as man is on God; when God unfailingly supplies man's needs, sending manna from heaven if necessary, man grows spoilt and forgets to pray. The charity of the Countess is surely a mirror of God's boundless charity, and the ungratefulness of the poor is that of man to his bountiful God. Dryden's overt panegyric on the Countess is also a description of God's charity and a comment on man's reactions to it. This double meaning in the poem enables us to see it as more than an exercise in flattery: it is also a vision of ideal Christian virtues. Mark van Doren disparagingly says: 'It is a catalogue of female Christian virtues, virtues which Dryden was not much moved by. It suffers from a threadbare piety . . .' If van Doren is right, *Eleonora* is a pretty bad poem. But is Dryden unmoved, and do his descriptions degenerate into a banal catalogue? Each reader will have to decide this for himself, but I can only say that the clarity of the thought, the unusual wit, the frequent simplicity of vocabulary, together with the

constant implication of larger issues, give the poem an attractive
air of alertness, of unsolemn seriousness. These next lines, for
instance, refuse to be spectacularly rhetorical: they are sober, neat
and modest, although they make such great claims for the
Countess. And of course they express Dryden's ideas on woman,
marriage, Adam and Eve, obedience to God and king, and so on.
As it happens, I do not agree with Dryden's ideas, but his lines
seem admirably succinct and deeply felt:

> A wife as tender, and as true withall,
> As the first woman was, before her fall:
> Made for the man, of whom she was a part;
> Made, to attract his eyes, and keep his heart.
> A second Eve, but by no crime accursed;
> As beauteous, not as brittle as the first.
> Had she been first, still paradise had been,
> And death had found no entrance by her sin.
> So she not only had preserved from ill
> Her sex and ours, but lived their pattern still.
> Love and obedience to her lord she bore,
> She much obeyed him, but she loved him more.
> Not awed to duty by superior sway;
> But taught by his indulgence to obey.
> Thus we love God as author of our good;
> So subjects love just kings, or so they should.

166–81

There are a number of up-to-date scientific images in this
poem, especially from astronomy. The effect is not merely of
novelty, I think, but of reminding us of the incredible magnitude
of God's universe—partly to shock us into humility, partly to
demonstrate that God's meticulous charity is the pattern for us:

> Thus heaven, though all-sufficient, shows a thrift
> In his economy, and bounds his gift;
> Creating for our day, one single light;
> And his reflection too supplies the night:
> Perhaps a thousand other worlds, that lie
> Remote from us, and latent in the sky,
> Are lightened by his beams, and kindly nursed;
> Of which our earthly dunghill is the worst.

75–82

This passage, and other allusions to the Milky Way or astronomical measurement of stars, help to expand the poem's frame of reference, so that we are led from a consideration of the Countess's idealised virtues to a recognition of God's infinitely greater charity.

In an elegy celebrating idealised virtues no doubt we miss the more passionate notes of grief or a personal evocation of the dead person, as one finds for example in Hopkins's *Felix Randall*. But Dryden's contemporaries probably appreciated the following passage, in which a subdued, witty treatment is used to stress the gentle, appropriate manner of her dying. The almost naïve manner of the verse makes her death seem a childlike ritual, dignified, but not over-solemn:

> As precious gums are not for lasting fire,
> They but perfume the temple, and expire,
> So was she soon exhaled; and vanished hence;
> A short sweet odour, of a vast expense.
> She vanished, we can scarcely say she died;
> For but a *now*, did heaven and earth divide:
> She passed serenely with a single breath,
> This moment perfect health, the next was death.
> One sigh, did her eternal bliss assure;
> So little penance needs, when souls are almost pure.
> As gentle dreams our waking thoughts pursue;
> Or, one dream passed, we slide into a new;
> (So close they follow, such wild order keep,
> We think ourselves awake, and are asleep:)
> So softly death succeeded life, in her;
> She did but dream of heaven, and she was there.

301–16

We may find it strange to see wit employed for such a scene, but I feel that it adds a delicate control over a description that could easily have become maudlin. Dryden is not inviting our tears: he is appealing to our sense of reverent wonder.

Finally we turn to Dryden's greatest elegy, the lengthy title of which is nicely informative: *To the Pious Memory of the Accomplished Young Lady Mistress Anne Killigrew, Excellent in the Two Sister-Arts of Poesy and Painting, An Ode* (1686). Anne was the beautiful daughter of the Rev. Henry Killigrew, almoner to the Duke of York, and she became Maid of Honour to the Duchess. She wrote poetry, drew and painted, and gained some reputation in court circles. She compared herself with the Matchless Orinda (Katherine Philips) and like her died young of smallpox. Dryden was a friend of the family, but may never have met her.

Two things strike us about this poem. First, only Stanza VIII is really elegiac; Dryden rightly calls his poem an ode, and there is far more joy than grief expressed. Secondly, how did Dryden dare to praise so extravagantly such a minor talent? He could not seriously have compared to Sappho and Plato the conventional young lady who wrote this kind of verse:

> My laurels thus another's brow adorned,
> My numbers they admired, but me they scorned:
> Another's brow, that had so rich a store
> Of sacred wreaths, that circled it before;
> Where mine quite lost, (like a small stream that ran
> Into a vast and boundless ocean)
> Was swallowed up, with what it joined and drowned.
> And that abyss yet no accession found.

Dryden wrote the ode late in 1685, the year he became a Catholic, and perhaps his new sense of faith and of his past sins is reflected in the contrasting passages relating to heavenly bliss, obscene literature and the Last Judgment. But, as A. D. Hope has so finely shown, the most unexpected thing about this 'elegy' is its use of humour. Dryden's seemingly excessive praise of Anne Killigrew's second-rate talent is continually being pricked by touches of irony, so that we are always aware that he *knows* she is no great genius. What in fact he is celebrating is the eternal art of poetry (in an age moreover when scientists and rationalists were denigrating the value of art), and Anne Killigrew deserves a share of this praise because, in her modest way, she upheld the values of art.

The opening stanza is a subtle blend of joyous Christian assurance, praise, and warning ironical smiles—'Don't take me too seriously!' Dryden whispers to us:

86

Thou youngest virgin-daughter of the skies,
Made in the last promotion of the blessed;
Whose palms, new plucked from paradise,
In spreading branches more sublimely rise,
Rich with immortal green above the rest . . .
Hear then a mortal muse thy praise rehearse,
In no ignoble verse;
But such as thy own voice did practise here,
When thy first fruits of poesy were given;
To make thyself a welcome inmate there:
While yet a young probationer,
And candidate of heaven.

'Promotion', 'probationer' and 'candidate' are all Christian terms, but, says A. D. Hope, 'the notion of the saved souls being "promoted" in batches is put forward with a grave smile', and the idea that the young poet and painter was 'on probation' on earth also reminds us that her talent is that of a beginner. Certainly the humour elsewhere in Stanza I makes delicate fun of Anne's heavenly choir-singing:

Whatever happy region is thy place,
Cease thy celestial song a little space;
(Thou wilt have time enough for hymns divine,
Since heaven's eternal year is thine.)

The next two stanzas appear to be fanciful praise of Anne Killigrew, for Dryden conjectures that her soul migrated through all the best Greek and Latin poets (and specifically the 7th-century lyric poetess Sappho) and of course her father, Rev. Henry Killigrew (the term 'traduction' refers to the theory that human beings beget both body and soul of their children). At her birth the angels played their lyres, the 'music of the spheres' was heard, and if no swarm of bees settled on her infant lips, as happened to Plato as a presage of his sweet eloquence, this is because heaven did not have leisure to repeat such a vulgar miracle! Surely nobody could take any of this seriously. It is fanciful compliment, beloved of the age. But the serious intention is to remind us of the ancient poetic tradition, and that poetry is literally a divine gift. (Some five years later Sir William Temple voices the current

87

man-of-reason's view: 'I cannot allow poetry to be more divine in its effects than in its causes . . .')

This leads in Stanza IV to a fierce attack on Restoration poets, including himself, for desecrating the divinity of poetry:

> O gracious God! How far have we
> Profaned thy heavenly gift of poesy?
> Made prostitute and profligate the muse,
> Debased to each obscene and impious use . . .

These are fierce accusations (supported by all his technical skill with explosive alliteration) and Dryden's imagery becomes astoundingly cloacal (or sewer-like) for such a poem:

> O wretched we! why were we hurried down
> This lubric and adulterate age,
> (Nay added fat pollutions of our own)
> T'increase the steaming ordures of the stage?

Lubric means oily, or lewd; *ordures* means excrement. The somewhat refined words veil the unpleasant scene. About this time Dryden was writing *The Hind and the Panther*, and did elsewhere voice shame at his own licentious verses. But surely he does not expect us literally to equate smutty Restoration Comedy with the Fall of Man, or imply that Anne Killigrew is another atoning Christ, as he does in the next couplet:

> What can we say t'excuse our Second Fall?
> Let this thy vestal, heaven, atone for all!

Changing tone once more, Dryden contrasts this prostitute literature with Anne's pure and simple achievements. He mirrors these by the short, naïve lines, as though he were imitating her own style. Her paintings are obviously conventional neo-classical concoctions:

> The sylvan scenes of herds and flocks,
> And fruitful plains and barren rocks,
> Of shallow brooks that flowed so clear,
> The bottom did the top appear . . .
> And perspectives of pleasant glades,

> Where nymphs of brightest form appear,
> And shaggy satyrs standing near . . .
> The ruins too of some majestic piece,
> Boasting the power of ancient Rome or Greece,
> Whose statues, friezes, columns broken lie,
> And though defaced, the wonder of the eye . . .

The impression is of pretty landscapes, packed with the usual neo-classical legendary bric-à-brac, and the final comment of the astonished spectator is not so much admiration as amused toler-ance—it *is* as quaint as Noah's overloaded boat!

> So strange a concourse ne'er was seen before,
> But when the peopled ark the whole creation bore.

The ode continues to vary its tones through the lamenting description of her death and the pathos of the allusion to her brother, a naval captain on a Mediterranean campaign, as yet ignorant of her death:

> Alas, thou knowst not, thou art wrecked at home!
> No more shalt thou behold thy sister's face,
> Thou hast already had her last embrace.

After this subdued note of sorrow Dryden startles us with a blast from the Last Trumpet, and stages a grandiose Heroic Drama of flying skeletons, poets leaping out of their graves, and saintly Anne Killigrew leading this singing throng to heaven:

> When in mid-air, the Golden Trump shall sound,
> To raise the nations underground . . .
> When rattling bones together fly,
> From the four corners of the sky . . .
> The sacred poets first shall hear the sound,
> And foremost from the tomb shall bound . . .
> There thou, sweet saint, before the choir shalt go,
> As harbinger of heaven, the way to show . . .

This is deliberately meant to be exhilarating, heady, gay even, so that the macabre spectacle of reunited bones and re-fleshed skeletons will appear exciting rather than gruesome. This particu-lar ode, celebrating both a simple young poetess and the eternal energy of divine poetry, could only end triumphantly, filling the heart with delight even as poets enrapture us 'with inborn vigour, on the wing,/Like mounting larks'. It is baroque theatre, operatic, dynamic, slightly comic, but impressive.

This selection from Dryden's elegies which we have been examining has a range of style and tone which we might not have expected. The elegy, like the panegyric, the epistle, the complimentary address, the ode, and other social forms of poetry, had a real function in 17th-century society. Unlike personal, confessional verse, the social poem celebrated some event or person for the benefit of a specific audience, and inevitably certain sentiments, certain styles, became customary. In our own day we can observe similar conventions in the tone and style of the public welcome to a visiting president or royal figure, in the stately and academically witty eulogies by university public orators on recipients of honorary degrees, or in the official verse of the Poet Laureate, who still feels obliged to write Coronation odes and so on. One does not take these social poems or speeches at their face value. As Dr. Johnson said of epitaphs: 'In lapidary inscriptions a man is not upon oath.'

In one sense the whole business is a form of social hypocrisy, the artificial cultivation of what today has become known as the 'public image'. Each man and institution offers an attractive façade, which it hopes will be accepted as an emblem of its true nature. Like advertising and propaganda it is really an ingenious kind of deception. Should we then abolish from poetry the compliment to a woman, the expression of grief to bereaved parents, or gratitude to a friend, or praise to an admired scientist or explorer? Society demands certain gestures, deeply sincere or politely conventional, as a means of maintaining standard attitudes towards social ideas. Dryden's age was very conscious of decorum, of the correct social gesture for any particular occasion. Before Charles I laid his head upon the block, he had to conform to the expected ritual of publicly forgiving his executioner, who kneeled before him.

Dryden, in his social poems, accepted the conventions of his day with, one imagines, little hesitation, given his conservative outlook and his deep desire for a well-ordered society. On the surface his poems could be seen as conventional tributes of grief and praise, degenerating into fulsome flattery or 'threadbare piety', and responsive to directives from the fee-paying patron or his own ambitious interests. This is a plausible interpretation of Dryden's work, but, considering here only the elegies, do the poems themselves read like the compliant outpourings of a mercenary talent? In the last resort we must look at the poems, not the circumstantial evidence, and decide on their intrinsic value. It seems to me that within the social conventions of his day and the current fashions for exaggerated, witty compliment, Dryden contrived to satisfy his immediate audience and patrons while at the same time celebrating those human values in which he so strongly believed. He was genuinely perturbed by Hastings's death. He found Cromwell's piety and energy admirable. He became a convinced royalist and Catholic, and gave his whole life to the service of literature; and his praise of the monarchy, or of Christian virtues or poetry springs from his deepest beliefs. We have seen that his eulogy of Charles, Eleonora or Anne Killigrew takes the form of barefaced exaggeration. This was the fashion of the times. But what he was praising was something genuine—an ideal ruler, an ideal Christian, an ideal of poetry. The notion that it is the business of poetry to present an idealised picture of reality, of what *should be* instead of what merely *is*, goes back to Aristotle, and Dryden himself subscribed to this doctrine in his *Parallel of Poetry and Painting*, when he said that painters and writers should form an idea of perfect nature, 'thereby correcting nature from what she actually is in individuals, to what she ought to be . . .' In Dryden's case, *we* have to dissociate the idealised picture from the reality which gave rise to it. We have to forget about the individuals, King Charles, the Countess of Abington and Anne Killigrew. If this seems grotesquely artificial let us remind ourselves that when we read a Greek tragedy we do not retain the ancient Greek's literal belief in those plays. And yet we can still be moved when a mythical hero addresses a mythical god. Dryden's poems are not valid as history, —whatever they were to him and his contemporaries—but as idealised pictures, as myth.

7

Verse Journalism: 'Annus Mirabilis'

Much of Dryden's work was inspired by national events or public controversies of his day, and his writing thus often has a topical ring and a wealth of contemporary allusions. It must have seemed excitingly up-to-date, full of famous names, discussing current problems and ideas—in fact, as fresh as the morning's news. We think that *Annus Mirabilis* was provoked by a series of similarly-titled pamphlets, which described horrific apparitions and prodigies warning the people of national disasters—fearful judgments from God on a wicked king and his government. Dryden hastened to refute these pamphlet attacks by writing this heroic account of naval victories against the Dutch, and by showing that the Great Fire of London had united the king and his people, who fight the disaster together and envisage an even greater London rebuilt on the ashes of the old.

In Dryden's lifetime there were a series of mercantile wars with Holland (and later France) as each nation struggled for new markets and control of the sea. Generally speaking, the king, Parliament and the City merchants were united in favour of these wars of economic expansion, as each stood to gain from them. (The Duke of York, for example, the heir to the throne, was Lord High Admiral, Governor of the Royal Africa Company, and a shareholder in East Indian stock.) Dryden's descriptions of the somewhat complicated sea battles are a blend of actual details and fanciful wit. The account of the events, horrible and heroic, is laced with ingenious similes and paradoxes, lending an air of artificiality to the passages. For example, when the English fleet attacks Dutch ships bearing spices from India, Dryden seizes upon the irony of death coming in the shape of scented luxury goods, which first betray the presence of the ships, and then murderously explode among the sailors:

> And now approached their fleet from India, fraught
> With all the riches of the rising sun:
> And precious sand from southern climates brought,
> (The fatal regions where the war begun) . . .
>
> By the rich scent we found our perfumed prey,
> Which flanked with rocks did close in covert lie:
> And round about their murdering cannon lay,
> At once to threaten and invite the eye . . .
>
> Amidst whole heaps of spices lights a ball,
> And now their odours armed against them fly:
> Some preciously by shattered porcelain fall,
> And some by aromatic splinters die.

ANNUS MIRABILIS, Stanzas 24, 26, 29

In addition to giving detailed reportage of the sea battles, Dryden is concerned to sustain a heroic tone and to please his readers with an ingenious style. Here are a few selected stanzas to illustrate how the horrors of warfare are somehow distanced by the stately stanza-form and language:

> On high-raised decks the haughty Belgians ride,
> Beneath whose shade our humble frigates go:
> Such port the elephant bears, and so defied
> By the rhinoceros her unequal foe.
>
> And as the build, so different is the fight;
> Their mounting shot is on our sails designed:
> Deep in their hulls our deadly bullets light,
> And through the yielding planks a passage find . . .
>
> Meantime, his busy mariners he hastes,
> His shattered sails with rigging to restore:
> And willing pines ascend his broken masts,
> Whose lofty heads rise higher than before.
>
> Straight to the Dutch he turns his dreadful prow,
> More fierce the important quarrel to decide.
> Like swans, in long array his vessels show,
> Whose crests, advancing, do the waves divide . . .

In the English fleet each ship resounds with joy,
And loud applause of their great leader's fame.
In fiery dreams the Dutch they still destroy,
And, slumbering, smile at the imagined flame.

Not so the Holland fleet, who tired and done,
Stretched on their decks like weary oxen lie:
Faint sweats all down their mighty members run,
(Vast bulks which little souls but ill supply).

59, 60, 65, 66, 69, 70

The realistic details about deadly bullets and sweat keep us close
to the battle, but 'willing pines' is too fanciful, and phrases such
as 'haughty Belgians', 'busy mariners' or 'dreadful prow' sound
bookish and unreal.

In fact, a rather stronger feeling of actuality is present in the
stanzas describing the repair of the damaged fleet. Dryden is
obviously fascinated with the technical terms of the shipwright's
craft. Indeed, he crams so many into the following passage that
perhaps it becomes clogged with them. But on the whole there
is a welcome homeliness and vigour reproduced as the din of the
shipyards and the smell of pitch are recalled:

So here, some pick out bullets from the sides,
Some drive old oakum through each seam and rift:
Their left hand does the caulking-iron guide,
The rattling mallet with the right they lift.

With boiling pitch another near at hand
(From friendly Sweden brought) the seams instops:
Which well paid o'er the salt sea-waves withstand,
And shakes them from the rising beak in drops.

Some the galled ropes with dauby marling bind,
Or cere-cloth masts with strong tarpaulin coats:
To try new shrouds one mounts into the wind,
And one, below, their ease or stiffness notes.

146–8

At least one critic has questioned whether an account of naval
battles, fought three centuries ago, can really hold our interest

today—especially when we realise that Dryden did not hesitate to rearrange the order of events or minimise certain shameful episodes so as to stress English courage and skill. The constant heroic tone (the English are always 'so brave a people' in contrast to 'the wily Dutch') rings too much like patriotic propaganda in our modern ears, nor can we easily share Dryden's naïve admiration for King Charles, 'the father of the people', who 'outweeps an hermit, and outprays a saint', and who seemingly takes a hand in sorting the ammunition:

> Our careful monarch stands in person by,
> His new-cast cannons' firmness to explore:
> The strength of big-corned powder loves to try,
> And ball and cartridge sorts for every bore.

149

Dryden is quite prepared to refer to Prince Rupert's arrival as 'this new Messiah's coming' and to envisage the heavenly angels peeping at the splendid English navy: 'To see this fleet upon the ocean move/Angels drew wide the curtains of the skies' (Stanza 16). Even the unfortunate incident in which the Duke of Albemarle 'lost his breeches to the skin' (to quote a contemporary) is turned by Dryden into a dignified heroic image:

> Our dreaded admiral from far they threat,
> Whose battered rigging their whole war receives.
> All bare, like some old oak which tempests beat,
> He stands, and sees below his scattered leaves.

61

The naval section of *Annus Mirabilis* includes a short history of navigation, for Dryden, like the scientists he must have met at the Royal Society meetings, was interested in the history of man's inventions. Dryden asserts that man first got the idea from fishes ('Their tail the rudder, and their head the prow'), then hollowed logs, added keels, then oars, then sails, and finally invented the compass. Looking ahead, Dryden sees science explaining tidal problems and thus in the long run commerce and prosperity will be assured to all:

Instructed ships shall sail to quick commerce;
By which remotest regions are allied:
Which makes one city of the universe,
Where some may gain, and all may be supplied.

163

Dryden anticipates that scientists will soon travel to the horizon
and take a closer look at the moon and planets (presumably
through the telescope developed by Galileo from about 1609):

Then, we upon our globe's last verge shall go,
And view the ocean leaning on the sky:
From thence our rolling neighbours we shall know,
And on the lunar world securely spy.

164

Many people in Dryden's day were fascinated with the idea of
space travel and wondered whether there were creatures on the
moon. As early as 1638, Bishop Godwin had published *The Man
in the Moon*, an imaginary voyage to that planet (where he
encountered men 28 feet high). Bishop Wilkins, a contemporary
scientist, published details of a winged chariot to fly to the moon,
and Milton's Satan in *Paradise Lost* (1667) makes some terrifying
journeys through cosmic space and even lands on the sun. One
description of Satan's departure in a cloud of smoke reminds us
curiously of the modern rocket leaving the launching-pad:

At last his sail-broad vans
He spreads for flight, and in the surging smoke
Uplifted spurns the ground, thence many a league
As in a cloudy chair ascending rides
Audacious, but that seat soon failing, meets
A vast vacuity: all unawares
Fluttering his pennons vain plumb down he drops
Ten thousand fathom deep, and to this hour
Down had been falling, had not by ill chance
The strong rebuff of some tumultuous cloud
Instinct with fire and nitre hurried him
As many miles aloft . . .

PARADISE LOST, Book II, 927–38

Dryden and many of his fellow writers not only praised the Royal Society and its scientific experiments, but also tried to make their poetry more scientific. Davenant, in his long poem *Gondibert* (from which Dryden took the stanza-form for *Annus Mirabilis*), banished classical mythology but devoted many lines to a description of a science museum. Some reformers became suspicious of all poetic imagery, feeling that an age of science should not tolerate such fanciful nonsense. (Bishop Samuel Parker, we remember, suggested that preachers should be forbidden by Act of Parliament to use metaphors.) But Dryden, and others, made a deliberate effort to use scientific imagery and allusions. So we find in *Annus Mirabilis* such lines as: 'Trade, which like blood should circularly flow' (a reference to Harvey's discovery of the circulation of the blood, published in 1628); or 'like vapours that from limbecs rise' (a limbec is a distilling flask); or 'like bodies on a glass . . . does its image . . . project' (possibly an allusion to the primitive magic-lanterns of the time). And even God quenches the Fire of London with up-to-date equipment:

> An hollow crystal pyramid he takes,
> In firmamental waters dipped above;
> Of it a broad extinguisher he makes,
> And hoods the flames that to their quarry strove.

281

We must not exaggerate the amount of scientific imagery in this poem. As Dryden reminds us in his prefatory letter to it, his main source of imagery was Virgil: 'my images are many of them copied from him, and the rest are imitations of him.' At times, however, it is difficult to tell whether an image has been borrowed from Virgil or more directly from scientific observations. Here, for example, the spider may have crawled from Virgil's *Georgics* but it is described as if under the fascinated gaze of a 17th-century naturalist:

> So the false spider, when her nets are spread,
> Deep ambushed in her silent den does lie:
> And feels, far off, the trembling of her thread,
> Whose filmy cord should bind the struggling fly.

Then, if at last she finds him fast beset,
She issues forth, and runs along her loom:
She joys to touch the captive in her net,
And drags the little wretch in triumph home.

180–1

The scientific interest in Nature is continued by later poets. Pope is to write on spiders, fish and flies; Thomson, in *The Seasons*, describes insects, insecticides, cattle diseases and sheep-dipping; William Diaper devotes scores of lines to the sex life of eels, tortoises, soles and lampreys. Dryden, at least, is one of the poets who pointed the way to this kind of verse.

The second part of the poem describes and comments on the Great Fire of London. Trevelyan, in his *English Social History*, tells us that the fire raged for five days and destroyed the whole of the centre of the city, the middle-class residential and business area, where many of the lath and plaster houses in the narrow streets dated from the Middle Ages. These houses and shops were rapidly rebuilt in red brick, safer and more sanitary, if less picturesque. Eighty-nine churches were destroyed, including the Gothic Cathedral of St. Paul's, thus giving Christopher Wren his great opportunity to construct new churches in the neo-classical style, often in white Portland stone. Unfortunately, the Fire did not touch the outer slum districts such as Whitechapel, Stepney and Lambeth, and in 1722 we find Daniel Defoe declaring 'they were still in the same condition as they were before'.

A first-hand account of the Fire is given by Samuel Pepys in his diary (that wonderful source-book for this period, written in a shorthand of his own invention and not deciphered until 1825). Here is part of his lengthy entries for September 1666:

> —Everybody endeavouring to remove their goods, and flinging into the river or bringing them into lighters that lay off; poor people staying in their houses as long as till the very fire touched them, and then running into boats, or clambering by one pair of stairs by the water-side to another. And among other things, the poor pigeons, I perceive, were loth to leave their houses, but hovered about the windows and balconies till they . . . burned their wings, and fell down.

—So near the fire as we could for smoke; and all over the Thames, with one's face in the wind, you were almost burned with a shower of fire-drops. This is very true . . . When we could endure no more upon the water, we to a little ale-house on the Bankside, over against the Three Cranes, and there stayed till it was dark almost, and saw the fire grow; and, as it grew darker, appeared more and more, and in corners and upon steeples, and between churches and houses, as far as we could see up the hill of the City, in a most horrid malicious bloody flame, not like the fire flame of an ordinary fire . . . it made me weep to see it. The Churches, houses and all on fire and flaming at once; and a horrid noise the flames made, and the cracking of houses at their ruin.

—Walked into Moorfields (our feet ready to burn, walking through the town among the hot coals), and find that full of people, and poor wretches carrying their goods there, and everybody keeping his goods together by themselves . . . drank there, and paid twopence for a plain penny loaf. Thence homeward . . . I also did see a poor cat taken out of a hole in the chimney, joining to the wall of the Exchange, with the hair all burned off the body, and yet alive.

Mr. Pepys, the immortal rubberneck, notices the pigeons and the burnt cat, seems annoyed at the profiteering on bread, weeps —but does not seem to have given the 'poor wretches' any assistance. His account is straightforward reporting—rough diary jottings. Dryden's method is quite different. His style is influenced by the fashionable 'wit' of a period which even liked epitaphs to be witty, and his aim is to draw an optimistic lesson from the seeming disaster. So it is verse journalism of a rather superior kind.

In the preface Dryden declares quite clearly: 'The composition of all poems is or ought to be of wit . . .' He then explains his neat theory that a poem consists of three stages: Invention (finding the thought); Fancy (variations on the thought, under the control of Judgment); Elocution (the art of clothing the thought in apt words). His recipe for writing poetry thus resolves itself into Thought, Variation, Stylistic Adornment. Let us watch him at work, using the recipe he has invented.

The Thought is the destructive Fire. A succession of stanzas, with Judgment guiding Fancy, varies the presentation of this thought in a series of personifications. We are meant to exclaim both 'How witty!' and 'How true!' as the changing images speed before our eyes.

First the Fire is likened to a usurper. (Oliver Cromwell, who rose from obscurity to govern England must here have sprung to the reader's mind):

> As when some dire usurper heaven provides,
> To scourge his country with a lawless sway:
> His birth, perhaps, some petty village hides,
> And sets his cradle out of fortune's way.

213

Dryden next mentions that the sparks are 'big with the flames' (an image based on child-bearing) and thus quite logically the conflagration can be called an 'infant monster'. This stanza captures the growth of the Fire (which probably started in a baker's shop in Pudding Lane):

> Then in some close-pent room it crept along,
> And, smouldering as it went, in silence fed:
> Till the infant monster, with devouring strong,
> Walked boldly upright with exalted head.

218

However, by the next stanza, the infant is 'like some rich or mighty murderer' who escapes from jail by means of bribery. Reaching the street, the Fire is pictured as a gallant, seducing courtesans:

> The winds, like crafty courtesans, withheld
> His flames from burning, but to blow them more:
> And, every fresh attempt, he is repelled
> With faint denials, weaker than before.

221

In quick succession the Fire leaps on his prey, opens wide his wings, feeds himself by means of his long necks (the flames) and even gives birth to a 'new colony of flames'. In Stanza 235 the fires are called 'curling billows' and yet they 'struggle up and down,/As armies'. These armies then divide into squadrons. For a moment the flames, amazed, 'stand gathered on a heap', but with military skill they lay bridges of smoke and proceed across them. Two stanzas later they are likened to 'dire night-hags' (or witches) and then to a hundred-headed hydra (the snake in Greek mythology whose heads, when severed, grew again).

This is not a complete list of the Fire's manifold forms. It wades the streets, eats its way, spreads like a contagion, peeps daringly into St. Paul's and finally, full with food, falls asleep. As we see, Dryden's Fire is personified as rebel, monster, murderer, gallant, army, hydra, and sacrilegious gaper, and many similes or images refer to a wide range of activities. This is what Dryden meant by variations on a thought and 'fertility in the Fancy'. There is no unity of simile or metaphor. The reader is intended to admire the technical *tour-de-force* of the inventive wit.

In newspaper reports of fires today we are used to vivid, often sensational, descriptions of the actual details witnessed by the reporter. We do not expect a 'witty' treatment in the Dryden manner. It is partly that modern taste differs from that of the Restoration period. But I think we may criticise Dryden on the grounds that the facile way in which he takes a simile and drops it a moment later, his rather showy virtuosity, in the end *reduce* the horror of the Fire. The technique becomes something of a game. We do not really identify the Fire with all that is evil in man and nature (which would justify the use of abundant personification and similes). We are merely, or mostly, struck by the ingenuity of the writer. Pepys's scorched pigeons and cats, described so simply, are somehow more moving. Nevertheless, the incidents themselves can still stir us: the terrifying march of the Fire, the attempts to halt it by blowing houses into the air, the plight of the homeless. And the descriptions of the fire-fighters with their leather buckets and brass hand-syringes intrigue us with their picturesque details.

Dryden's experiments in style are also of interest, especially if we realise that many of his suggestions were to become standard practice among the Augustan poets of the 18th century. He frequently personifies abstract things (such as 'gain' or 'luxury'), presumably to give them more life—but it must be admitted that it is often very difficult to picture a person at all. We are merely left with a rather empty, but obvious verbal trick:

> The diligence of trades and noiseful gain,
> And luxury, more late, asleep were laid . . .

(This means that the diligent, if noisy, tradesmen had gone to bed rather earlier than the pleasure-seekers.) Another device is to humanise Nature (here by making the sea or the fish behave in a human way):

> The wakened tides began again to roar,
> And wondering fish in shining water gaze.

It is puzzling to explain why we like to pretend that Nature behaves and feels like a human being. Primitive man presumably did believe in an animate Nature of this kind, but it is not easy to understand why poets, in particular, seem loth to dehumanise Nature (as the scientists have done). Dryden's attempts to lend human attributes to Nature often strike us as mere fanciful adornment.

Dryden is largely responsible for making much English poetry dignified and stately in the neo-classical manner (by, for example, his translation of the whole of Virgil). Of course, he and his educated readers were familiar with Virgil, Ovid and Horace because in the contemporary grammar schools children were taught Latin for most of the school-week, and the two universities still provided the old classical education—Latin and Greek. His readers could no doubt be expected to recall, when they read the following stanza, that in the *Iliad* the river Xanthus, calling on its tributary river Simois for aid, tried to drown Achilles and was attacked by Hephaestus in flame:

> Old Father Thames raised up his reverend head,
> But feared the fate of Simois would return:
> Deep in his ooze he sought his sedgy bed,
> And shrunk his waters back into his urn.

232

Pedantic though it may seem to us, the pleasure of recognising a classical allusion was, in Dryden's day and after, not as artificial as it now appears. Deeper still was the desire of poets to compare English civilisation with an ideal (perhaps idealised) standard of achievement.

Pope and other Augustan poets were very fond of breaking the verse-line in two and balancing each half rather neatly like a see-saw. Dryden uses this device often—here is a brief example:

> (Subjects may grieve, but monarchs must redress;)
> He cheers the fearful and commends the bold . . .

This can become something of a superficial trick, especially when the balance of phrase does not mirror any real balance, or poised oppositions, in the thing described. And too many see-saw lines make one a little dizzy.

Somehow we feel that the dignified language, which Dryden admired in Virgil, is not appropriate to describe the homely, and indeed pitiful scene of the houseless refugees, sleeping in the fields. The artificial style robs the episode of its moving human qualities. The second line in particular makes the distressing discomfort of the situation into something remote and unfelt:

> The most in fields like herded beasts lie down,
> To dews obnoxious on the grassy floor;
> And while their babes in sleep their sorrows drown,
> Sad parents watch the remnants of their store.

258

So whatever we think of the success or failure of these stylistic experiments, it is useful to watch Dryden at work in this early poem, which is something of an experimental laboratory in which various devices are given a trial run and tested for efficiency. From 1664 Dryden was a member of a Royal Society committee for improving the English tongue, and throughout his life he made pleas for a British Academy (to supervise the growth of the language). So presumably he was conducting these verbal experiments quite consciously. He tells us in his preface why he has used the *Gondibert* four-line stanza, rhyming a-b-a-b (which Gray later used with such a different effect in his *Elegy Written in a Country Churchyard*): 'I have chosen to write my poem in quatrains or stanzas of four in alternative rhyme, because I have ever judged them more noble, and of greater dignity, both for the sound and number, than any other verse in use among us.' Dryden obviously wanted to maintain a dignified heroic tone, but we may consider that this brief stanza disrupts the flow of the narrative. Like beads on a string (and there are 304 of them) each quatrain tends to be isolated from the others, even though the events described in them are continuous. At any rate, Dryden abandoned this form for his later poems, developing instead the heroic couplet, that is, two rhyming lines, which like bricks could be joined to other couplets to build a continuous poem— as long or as short as one pleased.

Annus Mirabilis is not a great poem, and its heroic view of historical events is probably not to our taste. But it is an interesting example of Dryden's verse journalism, of his experiments with scientific imagery, naval technical terms, personification, wit and so on. It teaches us a lot about Dryden the craftsman, and about his royalism, his patriotism, and his high hopes for English prosperity. Like any journalist, he had a story to tell, which he hoped would catch his reader's attention, but his aim in writing this chronicle-poem was frankly to praise, as he says, the 'prudence of our king; the conduct and valour of a royal admiral, and . . . the invincible courage of our captains and seamen'. Dryden used poetry as persuasive propaganda for a cause. He wanted to convince his countrymen that the naval struggles, the Great Fire, and the Plague (though he barely mentions the bubonic plague of 1665 which killed thousands of people) were not, as many thought, signs that God was dooming England to disaster, but a warning that Englishmen should unite around their king and work together for a bright future, based on naval power and expanded commerce. When the Fire threatens to destroy the naval magazines King Charles prays to God, who turns the flames aside and allows them instead to destroy St. Paul's Cathedral! Even God, it seems, wanted to encourage English naval might. Dryden's ideas about God's helping hand strike us as crude, and his praise of the king, the admirals and generals sounds to us too much like uncritical flattery. This is perhaps inevitable in a public poem of praise: one can hardly praise a hero half-heartedly. But whatever we now think of this type of poem, there is no doubt that Dryden really saw a brave new England arising from the ashes. This is indicated by the confident ring of the final stanzas, which picture London as the commercial centre of the world, with its mighty navy controlling the seas and its merchant ships sailing round the Cape to fetch spices from the East:

> Our powerful navy shall no longer meet
> The wealth of France or Holland to invade:
> The beauty of this town, without a fleet,
> From all the world shall vindicate her trade.
>
> And, while this famed emporium we prepare,
> The British ocean shall such triumphs boast,
> That those who now disdain our trade to share,
> Shall rob like pirates on our wealthy coast . . .
>
> Thus to the eastern wealth through storms we go;
> But now, the Cape once doubled, fear no more:
> A constant trade-wind will securely blow,
> And gently lay us on the spicy shore.

301, 302, 304

8

Satires

For most people John Dryden is the verse satirist of Restoration
England, who attacked his and King Charles II's foes in vigorous
heroic couplets, with biting 'portraits' and lively argument,
bequeathing to Pope and the Augustans an efficient verbal
weapon with which to trounce fools and fops of all kinds. Of
course, this is perfectly true, and perhaps this is Dryden's chief
claim to fame. Yet it is worth while remembering that during
his adult years, which spanned the second half of the 17th century,
he spent most of his time writing some thirty plays (comedies,
heroic tragedies, tragi-comedies, adaptations of Shakespeare),
translating Homer, Theocritus, Virgil, Lucretius, Ovid, Persius,
Juvenal, Horace, Boccaccio and Chaucer, and penning the criticism in prose which made him the founder of modern literary
criticism. So his well-known satires seem almost like odd marginal jottings in a lifetime of varied writing. They were in fact
published when he was fifty, within the space of two years:
Absalom and Achitophel in 1681, *The Medal* and *Mac Flecknoe* in
1682. *Religio Laici*, which we associate with these satires, was also
published in 1682.

The term *satire* defies definition, because the genre is extremely
flexible. There is tremendous variety in the form (in both verse
and prose) and in the intention of the writer. Invective, wounding
vituperation, didactic instruction, corrective ridicule, personal
abuse, pessimistic generalisations, mild scorn, amused raillery,
genial or sharp parody, slapstick humour, gross vulgarity, ironic
wit—one could compile an endless list of features found in
different satiric works. 'The true end of satire is the amendment of
vices by correction,' says Dryden, echoing a dozen other literary

critics, and though there is a general agreement that satire is a 'criticism of life', that it destroys by ridicule and, implicitly, upholds certain moral values, it is the variety of subject and style which dazzles our efforts to pigeon-hole the genre.

Scholars tell us (though they do not all agree on this) that *satire* has nothing to do with *satyrs*, but comes from the same root as *saturate*. Thus *satire* means a medley, or as Dryden said, a hotchpotch, and is a blanket-term like our modern *revue*. It was the only literary form invented by the Romans—by Lucilius (who flourished 150–102 B.C.). He was followed by Horace (65–8 B.C.), Persius (A.D. 34–61) and Juvenal (about A.D. 55–130, and publishing about A.D. 100–30). The Roman style of satire arrived late in England. Sir Thomas Wyatt (1503–42) wrote against court life. John Donne wrote three satires in 1593, and Joseph Hall published *Virgidemiarum* in six books, three in 1597 being 'toothless satires' based on Horace and Persius, and three in 1598 being 'biting satires' in the style of Juvenal. In 1598 John Marston published his bitter attack on Hall and others, called *A Scourge of Villainy*. But in June 1599 the Archbishop of Canterbury made an order that 'no satires or epigrams be printed hereafter', so that was that. (Satire is not a safe trade. Some Roman satirists suffered exile. Dryden was cudgelled by hired thugs in 1679. Voltaire was similarly treated in 1725. Some Soviet satirists have recently been jailed. Strict libel laws nowadays safeguard citizens from attack. Although Dryden attacked Shadwell, Shaftesbury, Papists and Fanatics he paradoxically objected to Whigs meeting in coffee-houses to swap witty abuse about the government.)

On the whole the Roman-inspired satire of this earlier period was too eccentric and obscure to be popular. Indeed some of the writers were deliberately obscure because they believed that this was part of the intellectual game the Roman satirists were playing with their readers. So Dryden could instead have turned for models to Chaucer (whom he later modernised) or to John Skelton (*circa* 1460–1529), whose jerky, short-line satires remind one a little of *Hudibras*. Here are a few lines from his *Elynour Rummynge*, a brewer of 'nappy ale':

Some wenches come unlacéd,
Some housewives come unbracéd,
With their naked pappés,
That flippés and flappés,
It wiggés and it waggés,
Like tawny saffron baggés . . .

Marvellous verbal knock-about farce, but not the model for the
Poet Laureate perhaps! Nor could the public poet, lashing
national vices, return to the precious satires of John Cleveland
(1613–58), who put ingenuity above all else—and described a
woman's hand as 'tender as 'twere a jelly gloved'. One wonders
whether Dryden knew of the satires of John Hall (1627–56), a
Cromwellian and a critic of current educational methods, who
entered Cambridge in 1646. At any rate his lucid couplets do
indicate the trend towards simplicity. Here he addresses a
prospective tutor in an aristocrat household and says to him:

[You] if some lowly carriage do befriend,
May grace the table at the lower end,
Upon condition that ye fairly rise
At the first entrance of the potato pies,
And while his lordship for discourse doth call
You do not let one dram of Latin fall;
But tell how bravely your young master swears,
Which dogs best like his fancy and what ears;
How much he undervalues learning, and
Takes pleasure in a sparrow-hawk well-manned.

Whatever hints Dryden took from contemporaries, such as
John Hall, Cleveland, Marvell, Waller or John Oldham, it is
clear that his classical education had early introduced him to the
major Roman satirists, and his later years are to find him translating them. And so, for good or bad, English satire once more
modelled itself upon Horace, Persius and Juvenal. When Dr.
Johnson wanted to describe Dryden's general significance for
poetry he said: 'He found it brick and he left it marble.' Perhaps
we have too readily assumed that Dryden, and Pope, likewise
perfected the Roman satire which they found and left it Augustan
marble. At least one classical scholar, Gilbert Highet, warns us

against this assumption. He tells us that 'all the Roman verse-satirists write in a bold, free-running hexameter, which has a range unequalled by that of any other metre except perhaps English blank verse at its fullest development. They can make it do almost everything from comical light conversation to sustained and lofty declamation'. On the contrary, the Drydens and Popes 'write in the stopped couplet—a metre capable of great delicacy and wit, but quite unable to attain a wide range of emotion, or a copious variety of effects'. He concludes that, compared with their classical models, they are 'severely limited'. Not only does Highet find in Dryden and Pope an over-indulgence in antitheses, but like the 17th-century French poet Boileau, they 'thought in couplets, and rode Pegasus on the snaffle'. Moreover, the forces of genteel respectability influenced Dryden somewhat (and Pope considerably), so that colourful slangy talk, eccentric vocabulary, or coarse abuse are replaced by polite innuendos or abstract terms. The verbal tricks of *Hudibras*, which Dryden disdained, are similar to some of the devices of the Roman satirists, and in refining his language and adopting the heroic couplet, Dryden also had to say farewell to the huge variety of Latin satire. (The gusto of his translations from Juvenal makes us realise the nature of his sacrifice.)

So Gilbert Highet really revises radically the usual view that Roman satire brought clarity and discipline to English satire, enabling Dryden, Pope and Johnson to produce English marble from English brick. Highet's detailed studies suggest instead that the English neo-classicists took the wonderful Roman hotchpotch and reduced it severely to the limited couplet satire that we know. Again, we can only test this view by experiment. If we are not familiar with Latin, then we cannot really make comparisons. But recent American versions of the Roman satirists suggest that we have for too long seen them through neo-classical eyes.

If we take Dryden's Zimri portrait, quoted on p. 123, we can find something similar in Horace's picture of the inconsistent Tigellius (in *Satires* I, *3*). Philip Francis's version, in 1747, has the familiar couplet rhetoric and gentility:

With this one vice all songsters are possessed;
Sing they can never at a friend's request,
Yet chant it forth, unasked, from morn to night—
This vice Tigellius carried to its height.
Caesar, who might command in firmer tone,
If, by his father's friendship and his own,
He asked a song, was sure to ask in vain;
Yet, when the whim prevailed, in endless strain
Through the whole feast the jovial catch he plies,
From base to treble o'er the gamut flies.

What a different tone is conveyed by S. P. Bovie's version (1959), which is far closer to the original in metre and detail of vocabulary:

The trouble with all singers is, when you want them to sing,
They're not in the mood, but when you just wish they wouldn't,
They can't refrain. Tigellius (a Sardine, not a dessert)
Was just like that. Even Caesar, who could have compelled him,
Got nowhere by pleading friendship, his own or his father's;
But if Tigellius felt in the mood, he would RENDER
'Yo, Bacchus!' complete, from soup to nuts, letting fly
With the high notes first and then rolling out the barreltones.
There was no *consistency* in him.

Horace's words: 'ab ovo usque ad mala citaret *io Bacchae*!' become the elegant 18th-century phrase: 'Through the whole feast the jovial catch he plies', which makes Tigellius' hearty rendition dignified rather than comic. Bovie's lines: 'he would RENDER "Yo, Bacchus!" complete, from soup to nuts' suggests Horace's irony, his detailed recapturing of the scene.

But though Dryden's balanced couplets taught the 18th century to refine the classics, he himself retained much of the earthy language and colloquial vigour of Roman satire when he translated Juvenal. In this passage from the Sixth Satire we find a blend of colourful diction and graceful rhythms: the coarse details survive, but the poise and smoothness of the couplets dilute Juvenal's harsh tone:

She duly, once a month, renews her face;
Meantime, it lies in daub, and hid in grease;

> Those are the husband's nights; she craves her due,
> He takes fat kisses, and is stuck in glue.
> But, to the loved adult'rer when she steers,
> Fresh from the bath, in brightness she appears:
> For him the rich Arabia sweats her gum;
> And precious oils from distant Indies come:
> How haggardly soe'er she looks at home.
> Th'eclipse then vanishes; and all her face
> Is opened, and restored to every grace.
> The crust removed, her cheeks as smooth as silk,
> Are polished with a wash of asses' milk . . .
> But, hadst thou seen her plastered up before,
> 'Twas so unlike a face, it seemed a sore.

The control, imposed by the couplet form, has its own attraction. It makes us feel the writer is coolly and ironically observing his victim. But the wit triumphs over the disgust. Something of Juvenal's brutal attack and moral repugnance is lost, though we can find it in Rolfe Humphries's 1958 version:

> Nothing is worse to endure than your Mrs. Richbitch, whose visage
> Is padded and plastered with dough, in the most ridiculous manner.
> Furthermore, she reeks of unguents, so God help her husband
> With his wretched face stunk up with these, smeared by her lipstick.
> To her lovers she comes with her skin washed clean. But at home
> Why does she need to look pretty? Nard is assumed for the lover,
> For the lover she buys all the Arabian perfumes.
> It takes her some time to strip down to her face, removing the layers
> One by one, till at last she is recognisable, almost,
> Then she uses a lotion, she-asses' milk; she'd need herds
> Of these creatures to keep her supplied . . .
> But when she's given herself the treatment in full, from the ground
> base
> Through the last layer of mud pack, from the first wash to a poultice,
> What lies under all this—a human face, or an ulcer?

Dryden's *Mac Flecknoe* has a certain vulgar buffoonery, and *The Medal* a ferocious humour, but his *Absalom and Achitophel* (together with his poems of religious argument) employs satiric portraits, or ironic commentary upon political and religious ideas, only as devices for the support of other genres. *Absalom and*

Achitophel is an ironic epic, or a didactic fable, though filled with satiric passages, and *Religio Laici* and *The Hind and the Panther* are poems of persuasion, laced with satire. As we look at some of these poems in detail we shall see how Dryden modified what he took from Roman satire or his contemporaries, creating really new genres within that vast hotchpotch called Satire. And there were still many more varied dishes, spiced with venom or wit or impudence, for Pope, Gay, Prior, Swift, Churchill and later, Byron, to concoct and serve hot. (An excellent anthology, significantly titled *Charitable Malice*, by Leonard Burrows and David Bradley, displays the riches of Augustan satire.) In our own century the South African poet Roy Campbell has continued this tradition in *The Georgiad*, a reading of which can give us an idea of the novelty and direct impact Dryden's and Pope's satires must have had for their contemporaries.

'MAC FLECKNOE'

Mac Flecknoe comes to us entangled in scholarly cobwebs. Some have doubted Dryden's authorship and it is now accepted that it circulated in manuscript in 1678, although it was only published in 1682. So it is his first, not his last, satire. (Osborn and Vieth argue that the poem was composed in 1676 or 1677.) Some have conjectured a personal, as well as a literary, quarrel between Dryden and Shadwell, the object of the satire, and the allusive nature of the poem has required its modern editor, James Kinsley, to aid us with some 400 lines of notes.

The allusions start with the title, and the sub-title is misleading. Richard Flecknoe, dramatist and poet, had been satirised for his hideous verse and comic figure by Andrew Marvell in *Flecknoe, an English Priest at Rome*, and for Dryden's contemporaries the name was now synonymous with 'bad poet'. The publisher possibly added the sub-title, 'A satire upon the true-blue Protestant poet, T.S.', leading us to expect an attack upon Shadwell's religious opinions. In fact Dryden does not even attack his moral character but confines himself to exposing Shadwell as a literary dunce. This supports the view of some critics that far from being a vindictive personal lampoon, *Mac*

Flecknoe is essentially a considered onslaught on bad writing by a man for whom literary values were sacred.

We are familiar with the television show which satirises another television show. It is highly amusing and topical for those in the know, and a bore for those who are not. Dryden's ridicule of a fellow dramatist has the same kind of specialised appeal. He alludes to scenes in Shadwell's plays, quotes bits of his dialogue, mentions the names of characters, and parodies lines from his epilogues. Added to which he imitates or burlesques passages from Virgil or Cowley, half-echoes biblical phrases about John the Baptist or, in the closing lines, bases a comic incident on Elijah's ascent to heaven. Unless you know that 'gentle George' was the nickname for Sir George Etherege, that Dorimant, Mrs. Loveit and Sir Fopling Flutter appear in his play *The Man of Mode*, and Cully and Cockwood in two others, you would not make much of these lines:

> Let gentle George in triumph tread the stage,
> Make Dorimant betray, and Loveit rage;
> Let Cully, Cockwood, Fopling charm the pit,
> And in their folly show the writer's wit.

Even so, mere identification of these names can afford little satisfaction: one would have to see the plays too. So a great deal of this poem is dead wood to the general reader.

What we can still enjoy is the mock-heroic verbal joke, the burlesque ceremonies, and the farcical incidents. Dryden considered it the first mock-heroic poem in English. 17th-century readers were very sensitive to literary style and found it highly amusing to describe a trivial incident in the high-flown language used to portray heroes and heroic deeds. Thus the opening lines have the grandiose, serious sound suitable for an epic theme. The name 'Flecknoe' warns us of the mocking ending in store:

> All human things are subject to decay,
> And when fate summons, monarchs must obey.
> This Flecknoe found, who, like Augustus, young
> Was called to empire, and had governed long;
> In prose and verse was owned, without dispute,
> Through all the realms of Nonsense, absolute.

The panegyric, or formal speech of praise, is a common feature of a heroic poem, and so with tongue-in-the-cheek gravity Dryden relentlessly presents Flecknoe setting his crown of dullness upon the only deserving heir, Shadwell. The aged prince,

> . . . pondering which of all his sons was fit
> To reign and wage immortal war with wit,
> Cried, ' 'Tis resolved; for nature pleads that he
> Should only rule who most resembles me.
> Shadwell alone my perfect image bears,
> Mature in dullness from his tender years:
> Shadwell alone, of all my sons, is he
> Who stands confirmed in full stupidity.
> The rest to some faint meaning make pretence,
> But Shadwell never deviates into sense.'

It is the solemn tone of a public oration which makes the ridicule so wounding. Dryden expands the original joke, alluding to Shadwell's enormous size, and mirroring the lethargic grossness of his body and the torpor of his mind in the oak image, which verbally sprawls across the page:

> Some beams of wit on other souls may fall,
> Strike through, and make a lucid interval,
> But Shadwell's genuine night admits no ray,
> His rising fogs prevail upon the day.
> Besides, his goodly fabric fills the eye,
> And seems designed for thoughtless majesty;
> Thoughtless as monarch oaks that shade the plain,
> And, spread in solemn state, supinely reign.

In a heroic poem there would have been a dignified description of the coronation scenes. The mock-heroic method employs grand terms, not to portray a king sailing splendidly down the river to the cathedral, accompanied by a royal orchestra (one thinks of Handel's 'Water Music' of a later period), but to suggest the bulky figure of Shadwell cutting his way down the Thames, to alight among brothel-houses and proceed to the Nursery, a theatre for the training of young actors. Despite obscure topical allusions the ceremony comes alive like a scene in a farce:

When thou on silver Thames didst cut thy way,
With well-timed oars before the royal barge,
Swelled with the pride of thy celestial charge . . .
Methinks I see the new Arion sail,
The lute still trembling underneath thy nail.
At thy well-sharpened thumb from shore to shore
The treble squeaks for fear, the basses roar:
Echoes from Pissing Alley, 'Shadwell' call,
And 'Shadwell' they resound from Aston Hall.

The modern hero's motorcade is greeted by ticker-tape and streamers. Shadwell's arrival is celebrated with sheets torn from unread books—material often used as lining for pie-tins or as toilet-paper:

Now Empress Fame had published the renown
Of Shadwell's coronation through the town.
Roused by report of fame, the nations meet,
From near Bun Hill, and distant Watling Street.
No Persian carpets spread th'imperial way,
But scattered limbs of mangled poets lay:
From dusty shops neglected authors come,
Martyrs of pies, and relics of the bum.
Much Heywood, Shirley, Ogleby there lay,
But loads of Shadwell almost choked the way.

The aged Flecknoe, a 'mighty mug of potent ale' in his left hand, feels inspiration raging within his breast, and blesses the reign of Shadwell in a speech which praises Shadwell fulsomely for attaining the summit of bad writing. Naturally the detailed references to Shadwell's plays and other literary matters of the day have little immediate impact now, but the gusto of Dryden's attack survives, and the final piece of low comedy as Flecknoe disappears through a trap-door makes an appropriate, stagey end to the poem:

'Heavens bless my son, from Ireland let him reign
To far Barbados on the western main;
Of his dominion may no end be known,
And greater than his father's be his throne.
Beyond love's kingdom let him stretch his pen;'
He paused, and all the people cried 'Amen'.

'Then thus,' continued he, 'my son advance
Still in new impudence, new ignorance.
Success let others teach, learn thou from me
Pangs without birth, and fruitless industry . . .
Leave writing plays, and choose for thy command
Some peaceful province in acrostic land.
There thou mayst wings display and altars raise,
And torture one poor word ten thousand ways' . . .
He said, but his last words were scarcely heard,
For Bruce and Longvil had a trap prepared,
And down they sent the yet declaiming bard.
Sinking he left his drugget robe behind,
Born upwards by a subterranean wind.
The mantle fell to the young prophet's part,
With double portion of his father's art.

Of course, *Mac Flecknoe* is great fun, despite the obscurities, and
Dryden's real purpose is to defend good literature against bad,
just as Pope was later to do on a bigger scale in *The Dunciad*,
which owes much to Dryden's poem. Whether verbal jungle
warfare really does keep writers and readers alert about literary
values I am not convinced: it is a hard matter to prove. It is
often said that satirists help to immortalise their victims, but do
they not at the same time prejudice us to such an extent that we
do not even glance at their work? How many who have enjoyed
Mac Flecknoe feel inclined to read Shadwell's plays? Are they in
fact worse than the plays of Southerne, Granville and Motteux,
which Dryden praised in verse epistles? We can only answer this
question by studying the plays themselves. We must not let
Dryden's persuasive ridicule distort our critical judgments.

'ABSALOM AND ACHITOPHEL'

Dryden's best-known poem is the supreme example of a masterpiece written to order, a topical piece of Tory propaganda
devised probably at the suggestion of Charles II himself, with
the specific aim of discrediting Shaftesbury and the Whigs. A
brief glance at the historical setting will show how 'occasional'
and partisan this satire was.

Queen Catherine had presented Charles with no children and

so the crown would pass to James, Duke of York, an avowed Catholic. The Whigs, led by Shaftesbury, wished to ensure a Protestant succession. In London they organised the burning of a mock-Pope in the torch-lit streets, with emotional demonstrations by chanting crowds. In Parliament they tried to change the succession by passing Exclusion Bills, that is, laws to exclude James in favour of the Duke of Monmouth. This popular Protestant contender for the throne was a handsome, ambitious, thirty-year-old soldier, capable, on a drunken spree, of helping to murder an innocent watchman. He was one of Charles's many illegitimate sons, and had been fathered in 1649, the year of Charles I's execution, when Charles II was nineteen. The Whigs suggested that Monmouth be legitimised by declaring that his mother and Charles II had entered a form of marriage, but Charles refused to support this lie. In addition the Popish Plot created a hysterical atmosphere, with Titus Oates leading the accusations that there was a Catholic plan to kill Charles and establish a Catholic state under the Duke of York. Sir Edmund Godfrey, J.P., before whom Oates's formal deposition was made, was found murdered in a ditch. Many Catholics and Jesuits were executed during the course of the Plot 'revelations', ending in 1681 with the deaths of Viscount Stafford and Oliver Plunket, the Primate of Ireland. Historians still differ about the true nature of the Popish Plot, and some now describe it as a Whig Plot to oust James and defeat the Tories. Dryden himself says, rather cautiously, of it:

> From hence began that plot, the nation's curse,
> Bad in itself, but represented worse.
> Raised in extremes, and in extremes decried;
> With oath affirmed, with dying vows denied.
> Not weighed, or winnowed by the multitude;
> But swallowed in the mass, unchewed and crude.
> Some truth there was, but dashed and brewed with lies;
> To please the fools, and puzzle all the wise.

108–15

Whatever Dryden really believed, it would have been too dangerous at the time to deny there was any plot.

The bitter struggle over the threatened Catholic succession was part of a much deeper conflict. The Whig and Tory parties were being formed at this time, with a considerable amount of political skulduggery on both sides, and the fundamental issue was whether the traditional powers of the king were finally to come under the control of Parliament. Dryden believed that an all-powerful Parliament could be as arbitrary a tyrant as an all-powerful king, for it could by voting change the laws of the land. He advocated a system in which the monarch should obey the constitution and Parliament should be obedient to the monarch, each subservient to the law of the land. This is a nice system so long as the laws are just and never require altering, and if king and Parliament consent to obey the constitution. To Dryden in 1680 it was clear that the main threat was of arbitrary parliamentary rule, supported by mob violence. He regarded the Whigs and the Dissenters as natural enemies of royal power, and in Shaftesbury he found a devilish, unscrupulous opportunist, a cynical manipulator of public opinion and religious prejudices. However, by 1681, the tide had turned in favour of the Tories, for the House of Lords defeated the second Exclusion Bill, and Charles dissolved Parliament. In March Parliament met at Oxford and voted for Exclusion again, but Charles dissolved it, and Shaftesbury was sent to the Tower on a charge of treason. His trial was arranged for 24 November, and on 9 November the Historiographer Royal published his *Absalom and Achitophel*. (Shaftesbury was in fact acquitted by a London jury. He fled to Holland, and died in 1683. In this same year occurred the Rye House Plot to seize the king, and many Whigs were tried for their part in it. The Earl of Essex committed suicide in the Tower, and Lord Russell and Algernon Sydney were executed. Monmouth went into hiding and in 1685 landed at Lyme Regis to lead a revolt against James II. He was defeated at Sedgemoor, and executed. Judge Jeffrey's Bloody Assizes took savage reprisals on his supporters.)

As Dryden saw it, Monmouth was being tempted by Shaftesbury to rebel against his father and rightful king. The parallel he chose as an allegory of this was the biblical story of Absalom's

attempt to overthrow King David at the instigation of Achitophel. (The account in II *Kings*, chapters 13 to 18, is not easy to
follow, and should perhaps be read in a modern English version.
In the Scriptures Achitophel's advice is not taken and he hangs
himself. Absalom, riding on a mule, is caught by the head in
the boughs of an oak, and is killed by Joab and others. David's
reaction to the news of his son's death is given in the celebrated
lines: 'O my son Absalom, my son, my son Absalom! would
God I had died for thee, O Absalom, my son, my son!')

By the time Dryden came to write his poem the parallel
between the Old Testament incidents and the contemporary
situation had been frequently made. Charles was often compared to King David, and Achitophel was a familiar term for an
evil counsellor. Dryden was not trying to be original; he was
using a story, and names, which already were loaded with
emotion—not to say prejudice. (Today we still can smear an
opponent by labelling him a Machiavelli or a 'little Hitler'.) In
addition the Old Testament framework lends an air of sacred
truth to the modern story, and gives the impression that man's
revolt against his king is constantly happening in history. Indeed,
as we shall see, Dryden's treatment of the biblical narrative subtly
suggests that this revolt is itself a parallel to the fundamental
Christian doctrine, that Man has revolted against God by sur-
rendering to the temptations of the Devil. (To give but one
example of Dryden's indirect method of hinting at the parallel—
when Absalom is described, before he is tempted, the notions
of 'grace' and paradisal innocence are incorporated in the
imagery:

> His motions all accompanied with grace;
> And paradise was opened in his face.)

And of course we must remember that to the 17th-century
reader the Bible was the most familiar and authoritative book
to which a poet could allude. (When somebody wished to warn
King Charles I of impending civil war he threw a stone into his
carriage with a paper bearing the message 'To thy tents, O
Israel!' A modern monarch would no doubt send this to his

decoding experts, but everybody in the 17th century would have recognised the biblical allusion.) So by suggesting the parallels of God—David—Charles II, Man—Absalom—Monmouth, and Devil—Achitophel—Shaftesbury, and equating the contemporary revolt against the king with the scriptural accounts of revolt by Absalom and Adam, Dryden had morally won his case even before he started. In an artistic sense he perhaps overloaded the dice. It is such a foregone conclusion that David—Charles II will win that the conflict hardly generates any tension. Nor is there any narrative action. Although the stage is promisingly set with semi-epical and satirical characters the plot dissolves into lengthy speeches. The dramatic events of Absalom's death and King David's weeping were not appropriate to the contemporary historical situation, so Dryden could not in any case have included them. The indications are, in fact, that he hoped for a reconciliation between Charles and Monmouth (whose wife, incidentally, had been and remained Dryden's patroness).

Most of Dryden's poems dazzle us with their opening lines. In *Absalom and Achitophel* the initial display of humour, seriousness and tact is masterly. It was essential to Dryden's argument to show that Absalom's illegitimacy was the basic flaw in the Whig case, but at the same time he had to persuade us to respect and sympathise with Absalom's father, the king:

> In pious times, ere priestcraft did begin,
> Before polygamy was made a sin;
> When man, on many, multiplied his kind,
> Ere one to one was, cursedly, confined:
> When nature prompted, and no law denied
> Promiscuous use of concubine and bride;
> Then, Israel's monarch, after heaven's own heart,
> His vigorous warmth did, variously, impart
> To wives and slaves: and, wide as his command,
> Scattered his maker's image through the land.

1—10

Most critics have praised Dryden's ingenuity in presenting the royal promiscuity as a genial excess of vitality in a period when polygamy was accepted, so that we feel rather prudish if we do not laugh at the amusing account of it. Dryden's enemies, noting his definition of Christian marriage as the cursed confining of one to one, plainly called him a cynical apologist for his royal patron. I think both views do injustice to Dryden's talent and his moral seriousness. As I read the passage, the tactful extenuation of Charles's behaviour is merely a ruse to allow Dryden to criticise the king's sexual sins and political blunders in begetting bastards. The whole passage is ironical, written in exactly the jovially cynical way Charles himself might have used to excuse his misdeeds. It only requires a little reflection to realise that, unlike King David, Charles II did *not* live 'before polygamy was made a sin', and that the cursed limitations of Christian marriage mirror libertine talk, not the viewpoint of an author who is going to base his arguments on the sanctity of divine and social law. The very frank terms 'polygamy', 'promiscuous', 'concubine', 'slaves', and the irreverent allusion to Charles scattering 'his maker's image through the land', are for a Christian reader (and author) impregnated with moral condemnation. Dryden gives us the clue with the first ironical phrase: 'In pious times, ere priestcraft did begin . . .' Is he really claiming that 'promiscuous use of concubine' is a sign of piety, or falling into his well-known anti-clericalism? Of course Dryden had to be tactful when writing about Charles, but I think he also had the courage to be critical, and the weapon he chose was irony. Like Chaucer's, Dryden's humour is clear-sighted and not indulgent to the follies it amusingly depicts.

The celebrated gallery of portraits offers us two groups—the 'malcontents' and the 'faithful band of worthies'. The main enemy, Achitophel, occupies Dryden for about a quarter of the poem, if we include his speeches, and the comments on him; and his portrait (lines 150–229) is mainly a moral attack, in the heroic 'high style', with little humour. He is too dangerous to be belittled by vulgar jibes. He is essentially evil, violent, changeable, as the lines insist with their piercing analysis of his deep-seated defects:

Of these the false Achitophel was first:
A name to all succeeding ages cursed.
For close designs, and crooked counsels fit;
Sagacious, bold, and turbulent of wit:
Restless, unfixed in principles and place;
In power unpleased, impatient of disgrace . . .
He sought the storms; but for a calm unfit,
Would steer too nigh the sands, to boast his wit . . .
In friendship false, implacable in hate:
Resolved to ruin or to rule the state.

150–174

I have omitted several lines with striking imagery to show how much of the satire is really direct moral denunciation. Though superbly organised, in jabbing phrases and with spitting consonants, such passages would become unbearably abstract and didactic without the inclusion of concrete imagery—especially the massy, physical imagery Dryden aptly uses to add a thick texture to the verse:

A fiery soul, which working out its way,
Fretted the pigmy body to decay . . .
And all to leave, what with his toil he won,
To that unfeathered, two-legged thing, a son:
Got, while his soul did huddled notions try;
And born a shapeless lump, like anarchy . . .

156–172

So what Dryden gives us is a moral portrait, enlivened by images which degrade Achitophel without reducing his potential for evil:

He stood at bold defiance with his prince:
Held up the buckler of the people's cause,
Against the crown; and skulked behind the laws.

205–7

The Duke of Buckingham (denoted by Zimri) had been a close friend of Charles II, and his chief minister, before siding with Monmouth. He had ridiculed Dryden in *The Rehearsal*, 1671. Like Shaftesbury he has real talents, but he is meddlesome rather than dangerous, for he dissipates his energies in a frenzy of interests—politics, chemistry, writing, sexual intrigue—squandering wit, wealth and life in the vain pursuit of pleasure:

> A man so various, that he seemed to be
> Not one, but all mankind's epitome.
> Stiff in opinions, always in the wrong;
> Was everything by starts, and nothing long:
> But, in the course of one revolving moon,
> Was chemist, fiddler, statesman, and buffoon:
> Then all for women, painting, rhyming, drinking;
> Besides ten thousand freaks that died in thinking.

> 545-52

Here the wit predominates, because Zimri can be dismissed as a political dabbler. Dryden himself called this style 'fine raillery' and likened it to the 'stroke that separates the head from the body, and leaves it standing in its place'. Indeed he thought the character of Zimri 'worth the whole poem'—which seems an exaggeration.

Passing from noblemen to commoners Dryden appears ready to descend in style from 'fine raillery' to derision and abuse. Shimei (Slingsby Bethel, sheriff of London) is dominated by his trading interests, which even triumph over his flaunted piety:

> Shimei, whose youth did early promise bring
> Of zeal to God, and hatred to his king;
> Did wisely from expensive sins refrain,
> And never broke the Sabbath, but for gain . . .

> 585-8

There follow detailed accusations of hypocrisy, seditious talk, packing of juries, and pamphleteering—all the sordid ruses of the king's enemies. Similarly Corah (Titus Oates) is subjected to withering contempt and personal abuse:

> Sunk were his eyes, his voice was harsh and loud,
> Sure signs he neither choleric was, nor proud:
> His long chin proved his wit; his saint-like grace
> A church vermilion, and a Moses' face;

His memory, miraculously great,
Could plots, exceeding man's belief, repeat;
Which, therefore, cannot be accounted lies,
For human wit could never such devise.

646-53

The rest of the portrait depends too much on biblical allusions to have a direct impact today, and neither the humour nor the invective is memorably expressed.

There is no specific character-sketch of Absalom. Instead Dryden rather ingeniously praises Monmouth as a likeable youth, manipulated by others, but allows him to reveal his rashness and ambition in his speeches. This is another example of his tact, and possibly he hoped Monmouth might be persuaded to reject Whig blandishments. ''Tis juster to lament him than accuse' says Dryden carefully. He does allow Monmouth to voice current Whig criticism of Charles in the reference to French and Dutch trading competition, Roman Catholic influence at court, the king's laziness, his acceptance of French bribes, his fondness for his mistress, the Duchess of Portsmouth, and it is even possible that Dryden agreed with this criticism, but it is significant that there is no fundamental accusation that the king is an arbitrary tyrant:

Now all your liberties a spoil are made;
Egypt and Tyrus intercept your trade,
And Jebusites your sacred rites invade.
My father, whom with reverence yet I name,
Charmed into ease, is careless of his fame:
And, bribed with petty sums of foreign gold,
Is grown in Bathsheba's embraces old . . .

704-10

It is at this point that Dryden steps forward and delivers his most formidable blows against those who would rebel against monarchs, sole guarantors of law, public order and private property. Fear of mob tyranny and radical changes is here expressed with resounding eloquence:

For who can be secure of private right,
If sovereign sway may be dissolved by might?

Nor is the people's judgment always true:
The most may err as grossly as the few . . .
All other errors but disturb a state;
But innovation is the blow of fate.
If ancient fabrics nod, and threat to fall,
To patch the flaws, and buttress up the wall,
Thus far 'tis duty; but here fix the mark:
For all beyond it is to touch our ark.
To change foundations, cast the frame anew,
Is work for rebels who base ends pursue:
At once divine and human laws control;
And mend the parts by ruin of the whole.

779–808

This dignified and powerful plea for conservatism shows Dryden at his most persuasive. However, one could reply that the state is not like a building. It can be radically altered without being destroyed. Indeed Dryden lived to see this happen in the Glorious Revolution of 1688.

Instead of plot or action the poem provides us with Achitophel's long speeches, tempting Absalom to rebel, and the final scene when the king speaks and asserts his authority. Without going into detail, one might simply say that Achitophel's dazzling rhetoric is beautifully composed by Dryden to suggest Shaftesbury's skill in argument, while at the same time clearly revealing the wily schemer at work. Here, for example, Achitophel's own words depict for the reader the murky tactics of the Whigs and Parliament (Sanhedrin) against the generous king:

Let him give on till he can give no more,
The thrifty Sanhedrin shall keep him poor:
And every shekel which he can receive,
Shall cost a limb of his prerogative.
To ply him with new plots, shall be my care,
Or plunge him deep in some expensive war . . .

389–94

In direct contrast to the tortuous reasoning, flattery and oily persuasion of Achitophel, the speech by King David employs a tone of confident finality. He extends mercy to Absalom ('But oh that yet he would repent and live!'), threatens his enemies with justifiable punishment ('Must I at length the sword of justice draw?'), and defends monarchical rule with vigour and satirical humour:

> That one was made for mercy, they contend:
> But 'tis to rule, for that's a monarch's end . . .
> Kings are the public pillars of the state,
> Born to sustain and prop the nation's weight . . .
> My pious subjects for my safety pray,
> Which to secure they take my power away.
> From plots and treasons heaven preserve my years,
> But save me most from my petitioners . . .
> The law shall still direct my peaceful sway,
> And the same law teach rebels to obey . . .
>
> 945–92

Throughout this scene King David is presented as a 'god-like' figure, and his speech is 'by heaven inspired'. When he has spoken, God is (rather too conveniently) at hand to display his divine sanction:

> He said. Th'Almighty, nodding, gave consent;
> And peals of thunder shook the firmament.
>
> 1026–7

Absalom and Achitophel poses an awkward problem for modern readers. Most people regard it as a striking achievement, and a unique blend of satirical portraiture semi-epical conflict, and didactic argument, and yet most people today do not share Dryden's strong royalist, conservative opinions. As one American critic has put it: 'From our point of view Dryden was on the wrong side.' How then can one unreservedly praise Charles's official propagandist, the Tory partisan who saw the complex constitutional struggles of the period as a black-and-white contest between a god-like king and a devilish Whig opportunist?

Various solutions to this embarrassing problem have been suggested. Some critics claim that Dryden was a moderate royalist who wanted both Parliament and King to obey the established law of the land, and so they find his attack on the Whigs understandable if exaggerated. Others claim that King David and Achitophel are type-portraits of the Good Ruler and the Evil Rebel, true symbols of the eternal conflict of Good and Evil in every period of history, but not necessarily accurate assessments of Charles II and Shaftesbury. Dryden's poem is therefore poetically if not historically true. W. Graham, for instance, refers to 'the timeless drama of authority and obedience, the battle between good and evil for man's mind'. But even a general statement such as this makes the assumption that man's mind is a battleground, containing two diametrically-opposed enemies. (Freud, for example, has a more complex tripartite concept of super-ego, ego and id, and many thinkers would hesitate to divide all the forces, inner and outer, which act upon the human mind clearly into two exclusive categories, good and evil.) In other words, I do not think we can extract truths from Dryden's poetry and ignore the context in which they appear. Even if we regard Dryden's *Absalom and Achitophel* as myth rather than history, as a diagnosis of human behaviour in general (irrespective of its historical accuracy), the resulting myth is still a product of his fundamental conception of life, just as the mythical tragedies of ancient Greece, for example, were impregnated with the notions that man was proud and life was unhappy. These are durable sentiments, but not necessarily eternal. Dryden's basic conception of life stemmed from the Christian belief in the Fall of Man, the battle between Good and Evil for man's soul, and the supreme role of the free-willing *individual* in this eternal conflict. That is why he saw the political, economic and religious struggles of his period in terms of *individuals*—not social forces, environmental conditions, fate, etc. (Now and again he accepted a current deterministic notion, as, for example, the belief that the temperate climate encouraged a temperate political system in England.) His Heroic Plays essentially present dominant individuals engaged in a moral struggle with opposing individuals. Practically every poem, be it panegyric, satire, ode, elegy or epistle, is concerned with an individual who has performed some worthy or unworthy deed.

Cromwell, Charles II, Achitophel, Shadwell, Eleonora, Anne Killigrew, Aureng-Zebe, Antony and Cleopatra are all larger than life because Dryden believed individuals were greater than the impersonal forces of society. The period as a whole was beginning to doubt this. Hobbes saw man as a creature doomed to live precariously amid a hostile natural environment. James Harington, in *The Commonwealth of Oceana*, asserted that *power* was the determining force in society. Descartes' and Newton's scientific works encouraged the belief that man and the universe were merely complex machines, governed by eternal laws of matter, over which the mind could exert little or no influence. Locke showed that the human mind was an empty slate upon which the external world wrote, thus creating each human being haphazardly, by means of sense-impressions conveyed mechanically from the outer reality. Seen in perspective, against the century's general trend towards the conception of man as a product (even a victim) of his environment, Dryden's stress on individual responsibility, individual achievement, and the elemental clash of good and evil, will appear old-fashioned even for its own time. His outlook is obviously Christian and, I think, must be judged as such. The non-Christian will presumably find it unacceptable. The modern Christian, if he is abreast of recent tendencies, will probably be sympathetic to Dryden's stress on the doctrine of the Fall and on individual free-willed behaviour, but will find his attitude to Good and Evil too simple. Christian thought today is striving to absorb into a new synthesis the hitherto unpleasant discoveries of scientists and materialists, so it is possible that to many Christians the complex history of Whigs and Tories, individual wills and economic forces, the subtle mingling of good and evil in public behaviour, would require a more sophisticated presentation than *Absalom and Achitophel* affords.

'THE MEDAL'

After imprisonment in the Tower of London, Shaftesbury was indicted for high treason in November 1681, but the sympathetic jury returned the bill marked 'Ignoramus' and he was released. For three days the London crowds celebrated this Whig victory with bonfires, and a medal was struck with a bust of Shaftesbury on one side, and on the reverse a view of London Bridge and the Tower, with the sun emerging through a cloud, and the inscription 'Laetamur'. Dryden's 'satire against sedition', again possibly suggested by the king, was published in March 1682, prefaced by an *Epistle to the Whigs*, in which the note of outraged anger is first heard: 'Never was there practised such a piece of notorious impudence in the face of an established government.' Dryden asks indignantly: '. . . what right has any man among you . . . to meet, as you daily do, in factious clubs, to vilify the government, in your discourses, and to libel it in all your writings?' He concludes that the fundamental heresy of the Whigs is that 'they set the people above the magistrate' ('magistrate' meaning the lawful ruler).

At this point in history the king's enemies seem triumphant, and Dryden reacts to the danger by abandoning fine raillery, and arguments for moderation, for a fierce attack on Shaftesbury personally, and a dire warning of a possible civil war. His scorn for the people and the Fanatics is more bitter than ever, and though he still employs humour as a means of denigrating his opponents, he also turns to straightforward polemical abuse. But it is not mere abuse. There are principles at stake, and the royalist argument is conducted with typical clarity. Topical allusions clutter the text, as we would expect, but editorial footnotes solve the puzzles for us—a labour-saving device for which we must be grateful. For example, we have to be told, to appreciate the opening lines, that Shaftesbury had once aspired to the elective throne of Poland:

> Of all our antic sights, and pageantry
> Which English idiots run in crowds to see,
> The Polish Medal bears the prize alone:
> A monster, more the favourite of the town
> Than either fairs or theatres have shown.
> Never did art so well with nature strive;
> Nor ever idol seemed so much alive:
> So like the man; so golden to the sight,
> So base within, so counterfeit and light.

One side is filled with title and with face;
And, lest the king should want a regal place,
On the reverse, a tower the town surveys;
O'er which our mounting sun his beams displays.
The word, pronounced aloud by shrieval voice,
Laetamur, which, in Polish, is *rejoice*.

1–15

From the outset Dryden expresses his contempt. Those who idolise Shaftesbury are like the idiotic rubbernecks who run to gaze at a fairground monster. (*Shrieval* refers to the London Sheriff, Slingsby Bethel, whom Dryden had satirised as Shimei in *Absalom and Achitophel*.) Shaftesbury's career is neatly sketched— soldier, parasite (*vermin* refers to earwig, a common term for one who whispers in the ear of a great man) and hypocritical Fanatic:

A martial hero first, with early care,
Blown, like a pygmy by the winds, to war.
A beardless chief, a rebel, ere a man:
(So young his hatred to his prince began.)
Next this, (how wildly will ambition steer!)
A vermin, wriggling in the usurper's ear.
Bartering his venal wit for sums of gold
He cast himself into the saint-like mould;
Groaned, sighed and prayed, while godliness was gain;
The loudest bagpipe of the squeaking train.

26–35

This portrait of a cynical opportunist is grimly satirical, not hilarious, for Dryden's aim is to wound rather than to raise laughter. He is equally serious in describing Shaftesbury's political motives, for Dryden is deeply convinced that democracy means arbitrary power in the hands of the people—or rather, their unscrupulous leaders:

When his just sovereign, by no impious way,
Could be seduced to arbitrary sway;
Forsaken of that hope, he shifts the sail;
Drives down the current with a popular gale;
And shows the fiend confessed, without a veil.
He preaches to the crowd, that power is lent,
But not conveyed to kingly government;

That claims successive bear no binding force;
That coronation oaths are things of course;
Maintains the multitude can never err;
And sets the people in the papal chair.

77–87

Dryden believes that only a monarchy can 'destroy the seeds of civil war', and he fears that Shaftesbury will drive England down the 'headlong steep of anarchy'. The monarchy, like God, is the check on man's wilful pride, and as he denounces sinful man, Dryden's tone changes to simple didactic condemnation:

God tried us once; our rebel-fathers fought;
He glutted them with all the power they sought:
Till, mastered by their own usurping brave,
The free-born subject sunk into a slave . . .
Ah, what is man, when his own wish prevails!
How rash, how swift to plunge himself in ill;
Proud of his power, and boundless in his will!
That kings can do no wrong we must believe . . .
Help heaven! or sadly we shall see an hour,
When neither wrong nor right are in their power! . . .
No justice to their righteous cause allowed;
But baffled by an arbitrary crowd.
And medals graved, their conquest to record,
The stamp and coin of their adopted lord.

127–44

Under the pressure of anger and fear the poetry forfeits some of its subtlety, and certainly its charm. One feels that the satirist is losing some of his control, and thus his air of superiority over his foes is threatened. Dryden's old confident ring returns when he asserts his faith in the positive values of monarchy, which he obviously sees as a constitutional not an arbitrary one:

For, in some soils republics will not grow:
Our temperate isle will no extremes sustain,
Of popular sway, or arbitrary reign:
But slides between them both into the best;
Secure in freedom, in a monarch blessed.

246–51

But serene passages such as this are rare. More typical are the ferocious attacks on Fanatics, the 'canting friends' who support the Whig rebels. Again there is more abuse than satire, but the anger for once finds true poetic expression in phrases bristling with consonants and stamping monosyllabic rhymes. The energy, clarity and wit can still hold us in lines such as these on the Fanatic sects:

> . . . the heaven their priesthood paints
> A conventicle of gloomy sullen saints;
> A heaven, like Bedlam, slovenly and sad;
> Foredoomed for souls, with false religion, mad . . .
> The swelling poison of the several sects,
> Which wanting vent, the nation's health infects
> Shall burst its bag; and fighting out their way
> The various venoms on each other prey.
> The Presbyter, puffed up with spiritual pride,
> Shall on the necks of the lewd nobles ride:
> His brethren damn, the civil power defy;
> And parcel out republic prelacy.
> But short shall be his reign: his rigid yoke
> And tyrant power will puny sects provoke;
> And frogs and toads, and all the tadpole train
> Will croak to heaven for help, from this devouring crane.

283–305

9

Poems of Persuasion

The 17th century had a huge appetite for religious controversy. The presses yearly disgorged weighty volumes on abstruse points of doctrine in which dry-as-dust niggling scholarship was often imbedded in purple passages of indignant abuse. By a sort of chain-reaction process each pamphlet produced a reply, then a defence of the original, then a refutation of the defence, then an animadversion against the refutation of the defence, and so on! It is easy to sneer at this frenzied battle of the books, or smile at such quaint titles as *The Backparts of Jehova*, or *Bowels Opened*, but this ideological warfare reflected a serious concern with Christian belief. In Dryden's day the sharp tension between Anglicans, Catholics and Dissenters was complicated by the growth of scepticism and deism (natural religion, or belief in a god without an acceptance of revelation). Religious differences aroused strong political passions because Dissent was allied to Whig demands for increased parliamentary power; Anglicanism defended the Protestant monarchy; and Catholicism looked forward to the succession of the Catholic Duke of York to the throne. To their enemies the Dissenters were potential republicans, dreaming of a new Cromwellian-type régime; the Anglicans were accused of using their national church to persecute non-conformists; the Catholics were suspected of Popish Plots to assassinate the king and re-establish the Roman faith by force.

'RELIGIO LAICI'

A year after he had, in *Absalom and Achitophel*, defended the monarchy against Shaftesbury, and three years before he openly adopted Catholicism, Dryden, in November 1682, entered the field with his *Religio Laici or A Layman's Faith*—though it did not attract a great deal of attention. The poem was inspired by the translation of Father Simon's pro-Catholic *Histoire Critique du Vieux Testament* by Dryden's friend Henry Dickenson. Simon's book threw doubt on the reliability of biblical manuscripts, and caused great anxiety among orthodox Anglicans. But earlier there had been a series of pamphlets, such as Martin Clifford's *A Treatise of Human Reason*, and *Religio Clerici* by a clergyman, which sharply debated the roles of reason and revelation in Christian belief. Dryden's poem seems to be an attempt to offer a layman's solution to a controversy which threatened both the religious and political life of the nation. The ironic thing is that modern critics cannot agree on what Dryden meant to say! Louis I. Bredvold insists that Dryden was an extreme philosophical sceptic who, in despair of finding truth through reason, was driven to accept the authority of the Catholic Church. He sees *Religio Laici* not as a defence of Anglicanism so much as the revelation of Dryden's nearness to Catholicism. On the other hand, Edward N. Hooker claims Dryden was a moderate sceptic, attacking dogmatism in Puritans, Catholics and materialists, whereas Elias J. Chiasson dubs him a Christian Humanist preserving the Anglican traditional balance between faith and reason. Dryden may have intended to put a stop to a heated 17th-century controversy, but in doing so he has caused a 20th-century controversy about his own views.

Dryden's preface repeats much of the argument of the poem. He certainly says he is 'naturally inclined to scepticism in philosophy'. He regards natural religion, or deism, as 'the faint remnants or dying flames of revealed religion', and on the question of reason and faith it is clear that he is no rationalist: 'They who would prove religion by reason do but weaken the cause which they endeavour to support: 'tis to take away the pillars from our faith, and to prop it only with a twig . . .' He attacks the papal claim to infallibility as well as the 'infallibility in the private spirit' of the puritan sects (Dryden calls them Fanatics), although he sees the Fanatics as politically more threatening than the Papists, of whom he says rather carefully: 'I think them the

less dangerous, at least in appearance, to our present state . . .'
Dryden feared that the Jesuits would support the deposing, and
even assassination, of 'heretical' King Charles, and that the
Fanatics who had executed Charles I were ever ready to start a
new rebellion. Each group found support for its actions in the
Bible: the holy manual of obedience to one's rulers had become a
guide book for rebels. Dryden's proposals to Papists and Fanatics
are perhaps ironical rather than naïve: he asks Catholics to 'join
in a public act of disowning and detesting these Jesuitic principles'
and he tells the Fanatics 'to disclaim their principles and renounce
their practices', for 'we shall all be glad to think them true
Englishmen when they obey the king, and true Protestants when
they conform to the Church discipline'. Although there were, in
the 17th century, some voices genuinely advocating toleration of
diverging views, 'agreeing to differ' as we now say, Dryden's
was not one of them. His attitude, persuasively argued, was
simply: 'Let's be reasonable: why don't you all conform to my
views? You are extremists: I stand sensibly in the middle. For the
sake of public order, let's sacrifice our prejudices and unite
around a single creed that even a layman can understand.'
Dryden did not exactly take his own advice. Three years later he
became a Catholic.

The preface ends with a note on the style Dryden has adopted
for a poem 'designed purely for instruction'. The heroic mode
would not be suitable, and so he has imitated the *Epistles* of
Horace, aiming to be 'plain and natural, and yet majestic'.
Significantly, Dryden regards the 'florid, elevated, and figurative
way' of heroic poetry as a means of stirring the reader's passions,
and he adds: 'A man is to be cheated into passion, but to be
reasoned into truth.' That the poetry of metaphor and emotion
is somehow a 'cheat' shows how near Dryden sometimes came to
sharing the 18th-century suspicion that fancy and feeling were
untruthful. As we shall see, his style in *Religio Laici* is not as
unadorned and prosaic as he claims at the end of the poem:

And this unpolished, rugged verse, I chose,
As fittest for discourse, and nearest prose . . .

The poem indeed opens majestically, but not prosaically, with a metaphorical statement about reason and faith, comparing them with the moon and the sun as sources of light (which is possibly based on a passage in Donne's *Biathanatos*):

> Dim as the borrowed beams of moon and stars
> To lonely, weary, wandering travellers,
> Is Reason to the soul; and, as on high
> Those rolling fires discover but the sky,
> Not light us here, so Reason's glimmering ray
> Was lent, not to assure our doubtful way,
> But guide us upward to a better day.
> And as those nightly tapers disappear,
> When day's bright lord ascends our hemisphere;
> So pale grows Reason at Religion's sight;
> So dies, and so dissolves in supernatural light.

1–11

This is not irrationalism: Reason has its role as a guide. But it must dissolve into the superior spiritual light of Faith. This is Dryden's position throughout, as he attacks various abuses of Reason.

Four modes of human thinking are shown to have failed. The great philosophical systems of Aristotle and Epicurus were merely guesswork. There was no certainty in their belief, and they were unable to find a true design for mortal happiness, for the human mind cannot comprehend the superhuman:

> Thus anxious thoughts in endless circles roll,
> Without a centre where to fix the soul;
> In this wild maze their vain endeavours end:
> How can the less the greater comprehend?
> Or finite Reason reach Infinity?
> For what could fathom God were more than He.

36–41

A large portion of the poem is devoted to a criticism of Deism, which, says Dryden, asserts that solely by his Reason man can deduce that there is a God and a future state. Thus, the various religions, with their individual creeds and rituals, are superstitious trappings which Reason can dispense with. Dryden's main retort is that what is true in Deism is simply borrowed from the Christian revelation without acknowledgement:

> Vain, wretched creature, how art thou misled
> To think thy wit these godlike notions bred!
> These truths are not the product of thy mind,
> But dropped from heaven, and of a nobler kind.
> Revealed Religion first informed thy sight,
> And Reason saw not, till Faith sprung the light.
> Hence all thy natural worship takes the source:
> 'Tis revelation what thou thinkst discourse.

64–71

Dryden continues by affirming the validity of the Scriptures as our source of revelation. They are divinely inspired:

> Whence, but from heaven, could men unskilled in arts,
> In several ages born, in several parts,
> Weave such agreeing truths? or how, or why,
> Should all conspire to cheat us with a lie?

140–3

History confirms the Christian story, and miracles support the Christian doctrine:

> Concurrent heathens prove the story true;
> The doctrine, miracles; which must convince,
> For heaven in them appeals to human sense ...

147–9

And the biblical style itself convinces us that God himself is speaking:

> Then for the style; majestic and divine,
> It speaks no less than God in every line ...

152–3

In other words—the Bible must come from God because it sounds so godlike! Dryden's argument is full of this question-begging half-logic which we all find so terribly convincing—especially if we already agree with the propositions!

After reviewing Father Simon's picture of scriptural textual corruptions, which he seems to accept, Dryden then naturally turns to that kind of Reason which places excessive reliance on tradition—that is, Christian records, written and oral. If the careful and reverent Jewish theologians

> Let in gross errors to corrupt the text,
> Omitted paragraphs, embroiled the sense . . .

265–6

how can Reason be so dogmatic as to claim certainty in an area where human error can grow? And the oral tradition (particularly dear to Catholics) is even less certain:

> If written words from time are not secured,
> How can we think have oral sounds endured?

270–1

Dryden's scepticism here brings him close to despair of ever discovering 'an unerring guide'. The phrase prompts him to think of the Catholic claim to infallibility in the interpretation of Church tradition, and he exclaims:

> Such an omniscient Church we wish indeed;
> 'Twere worth both Testaments; and cast in the Creed . . .

282–3

These lines have caused Bredvold and others to assert that Dryden here voices his yearning for the unshakable authority of the Catholic Church, but surely the tone is ironical? The crude image of the Bible and Creed being tossed (in a balance?) in return for infallibility is hardly reverent, and the passage continues by sharply reminding us that the infallible guide cannot in fact even tell which texts are corrupt. Dryden's conclusion is the apparently common-sense one that the Bible is imperfect, but perfect enough on the main issues. We must believe:

> God would not leave mankind without a way;
> And that the Scriptures, though not everywhere
> Free from corruption, or entire, or clear,
> Are uncorrupt, sufficient, clear, entire,
> In all things which our needful faith require.

296–300

Dryden is really rather ingenious! The corrupt bits of the Bible are not really the important bits! After all, God would not leave man in such a muddle! And so there is the strong tendency in this poem to sidestep theological problems by asserting that the ordinary Christian need not bother about them. In fact, obscure points are most probably minor matters. The main points are always clear:

> Th'unlettered Christian, who believes in gross,
> Plods on to heaven, and ne'er is at a loss;
> For the strait gate would be made straiter yet,
> Were none admitted there but men of wit . . .
> 'Tis some relief that points not clearly known
> Without much hazard may be let alone . . .

322 . . . 444

In considering Papist claims Dryden's imagination suddenly takes wing, and one of the most vigorous passages is this irreverent account of Catholic exploitation of the monopoly of knowledge. The shopkeeping metaphors and the breezy colloquialisms are far from the plain yet majestic style he had promised:

> In times o'ergrown with rust and ignorance,
> A gainful trade their clergy did advance;
> When want of learning kept the laymen low,
> And none but priests were authorised to know;
> When what small knowledge was, in them did dwell,
> And he a god who could but read or spell:
> Then Mother Church did mightily prevail;
> She parcelled out the bible by retail;
> But still expounded what she sold or gave,
> To keep it in her power to damn and save:
> Scripture was scarce, and, as the market went,
> Poor laymen took salvation on content;
> As needy men take money, good or bad:
> God's word they had not, but the priest's they had . . .
> In those dark times they learned their knack so well,
> That by long use they grew infallible . . .

370–87

Similarly, when Dryden describes the fourth abuse of Reason, the equally dogmatic claim of Fanatics to be ruled by nothing but their 'private spirit', 'conscience' or 'inner light', his satiric fancy again produces picturesque farcical detail, raised by wit and verbal devices into a comic but pungent attack. The Catholic's greedy monopoly of the Bible was broken, only to result in the mob anarchy of every man his own church:

> The book thus put in every vulgar hand,
> Which each presumed he best could understand,
> The common rule was made the common prey,
> And at the mercy of the rabble lay.
> The tender page with horny fists was galled,
> And he was gifted most that loudest bawled:
> The spirit gave the doctoral degree;
> And every member of a company
> Was of his trade and of the bible free . . .
> Study and pains were now no more their care;
> Texts were explained by fasting and by prayer:
> This was the fruit the private spirit brought,
> Occasioned by great zeal and little thought.
> While crowds unlearned, with rude devotion warm,
> About the sacred viands buzz and swarm,
> The fly-blown text creates a crawling brood,
> And turns to maggots what was meant for food.
> A thousand daily sects rise up and die;
> A thousand more the perished race supply . . .

400—22

Although this Fanatic enthusiasm (denigrated by the allusions to horny fists or maggots) manifests itself as *lack* of Reason, basing itself on grace without knowledge, it is an abuse of Reason in that it ultimately springs from a dogmatic belief that each man has his own powers of reason, valid for him, and his surest guide, even if Church or Tradition are opposed.

Dryden's conclusion is not unexpected. Amid the errors of extremists, deistical, papist or fanatical, there must be a golden mean, a way simple enough for the layman:

> What then remains, but, waiving each extreme,
> The tides of ignorance and pride to stem? . . .
> Faith is not built on disquisitions vain;
> The things we must believe are few and plain . . .

427—32

The calm tone helps us to find this view comforting. And if some men will insist on believing 'more than they need' it would be better to consult the safer ancient authorities on theology than their own private Reason. And Dryden's final plea is not religious at all, but political. For the sake of public peace religious enthusiasms should be curbed:

> If still our Reason runs another way,
> That private Reason 'tis more just to curb,
> Than by disputes the public peace disturb.
> For points obscure are of small use to learn;
> But common quiet is mankind's concern.

446–50

This sounds like religious indifferentism, putting political order before the demands of Christian conscience. But remember, in November 1682, when *Religio Laici* appeared, England was still suffering the hysteria of the Popish Plot, which brought a wave of terror and executions.

'THE HIND AND THE PANTHER'

In 1685 King James II succeeded to the throne and Dryden openly espoused Catholicism. In the winter of 1686 he composed his lengthy fable *The Hind and the Panther*, in three parts, which consists mainly of a disputation between a 'milk white Hind, immortal and unchanged' (the Catholic Church) and a female Panther (the Church of England) about the history of schism, papal infallibility and transubstantiation, as well as such topical matters as the Test Act, James's policy, Huguenot refugees and so on. I think nobody has been kind about Dryden's use of wolves, panthers and poultry to portray Christian denominations—he almost apologises for it himself in part three—and Dr. Johnson's laconic irony is typical: 'The Hind at one time is afraid to drink at the common brook, because she may be worried; but walking home with the Panther, talks by the way of the Nicene Fathers, and at last declares herself to be the Catholic Church.' Beast fables were very popular in the Middle Ages, but unlike Chaucer with Chauntecleer and Pertelote, Dryden has to take his Hind

and Panther seriously. Where he is able to introduce humour,
even of a savage kind, as in his picture of fanatical sects, we are
happy to accept the animal allegory. His old satirical touch does
not desert him in his ferocious attack on Independents, Quakers
and Baptists:

> The bloody Bear an Independent beast,
> Unlicked to form, in groans her hate expressed.
> Among the timorous kind the Quaking Hare
> Professed neutrality, but would not swear . . .
> The bristled Baptist Boar, impure as he,
> (But whitened with the foam of sanctity)
> With fat pollutions filled the sacred place . . .

I, 35 . . . 45

More lines are devoted to the Presbyterian Wolf, which Dryden
regards as highly dangerous. But there are some comic asides, as
in the clever allusion to the doctrine of predestination by reference to the way the Presbyterian black skull-cap made the ears
project, giving rise to the nickname of Prick-eared Fanatics:

> More haughty than the rest the wolfish race,
> Appear with belly gaunt and famished face:
> Never was so deformed a beast of Grace.
> His ragged tail betwixt his legs he wears
> Close clapped for shame, but his rough crest he rears,
> And pricks up his predestinating ears.

I, 160-5

Lion of course signifies king, but in the case of Henry VIII,
founder of the Anglican Church, the royal portrait is unsym-
pathetic:

> A Lion old, obscene, and furious made
> By lust, compressed her mother in a shade.
> Then, by a left-hand marriage weds the dame,
> Covering adultery with a specious name:
> So schism begot; and sacrilege and she,
> A well-matched pair, got graceless heresy.

I, 351-6

Dryden's personal and political venom inspires the portrait of
King Buzzard, the historian (and later Bishop) Gilbert Burnet

who harried James's recatholicising policy and offended Dryden in print. Hatred is mixed with that satiric gusto which makes Dryden's verse so enjoyable even when he is trying to be unpleasant:

> A portly prince, and goodly to the sight,
> He seemed a son of Anach for his height:
> Like those whom stature did to crowns prefer;
> Black-browed, and bluff, like Homer's Jupiter:
> Broad-backed, and brawny built for love's delight,
> A prophet formed, to make a female proselyte ...
> Prompt to assail, and careless of defence,
> Invulnerable in his impudence;
> He dares the world, and eager of a name,
> He thrusts about, and jostles into fame.
> Frontless, and satire-proof he scours the streets,
> And runs an Indian muck at all he meets.
> So fond of loud report, that not to miss
> Of being known (his last and utmost bliss)
> He rather would be known, for what he is.

III, 1141 ... 91

In contrast to the comic energy of such passages we have the serious and more elegant descriptions of the Catholic and Anglican Churches. The Hind is persecuted but ordained never to die:

> A milk white Hind, immortal and unchanged,
> Fed on the lawns, and in the forest ranged;
> Without unspotted, innocent within,
> She feared no danger, for she knew no sin.
> Yet had she oft been chased with horns and hounds,
> And Scythian shafts; and many winged wounds
> Aimed at her heart; was often forced to fly,
> And doomed to death, though fated not to die.

I, 1–8

Probably Dryden shared the view that Catholics and Anglicans might be persuaded to reunite under King James, and his lines on the Panther seem to soften criticism with praise:

The Panther sure the noblest, next the Hind,
And fairest creature of the spotted kind;
Oh, could her inborn stains be washed away,
She were too good to be a beast of prey!
How can I praise, or blame, and not offend,
Or how divide the frailty from the friend!
Her faults and virtues lie so mixed, that she
Nor wholly stands condemned, nor wholly free.

I, 327–34

Once the animals have been introduced there is little action, and
the lack of narrative interest is not compensated by the long
theological discussion. Dryden makes a feeble attempt to
dramatise the debate by mentioning that one or the other smiles,
or grins. With a show of fairness he allows the Panther to throw
a certain amount of mud at the Hind, but there is never any
doubt that the Hind will find a crushing retort. It is a mock-
battle staged by one who has strong partisan convictions. The
question of scriptural authority, oral tradition, and the role of
reason and faith, are those handled in *Religio Laici*, but now
Dryden is convinced that only the Catholic Church can provide
the 'unerring guide' which he deeply needs:

But, gracious God, how well dost thou provide
For erring judgements an unerring guide?
Thy throne is darkness in th'abyss of light,
A blaze of glory that forbids the sight;
O teach me to believe thee thus concealed,
And search no farther than thyself revealed;
But her alone for my director take
Whom thou hast promised never to forsake!

I, 64–71

Dryden's hatred of Fanatics is now quite implacable and his
opposition to all forms of rebellion, political or religious, is
stronger than ever. Protestantism is rebellion against the Mother
Church and therefore constantly encourages political rebellion.
Only Catholicism can teach absolute obedience to God and
King. Clarity of argument joins with confident faith in such
passages as this, describing the Catholic Church:

> One in herself, not rent by schism, but sound,
> Entire, one solid shining diamond,
> Not sparkles shattered into sects like you,
> One is the church, and must be to be true:
> One central principle of unity.

II, 526–30

Where there is deep feeling behind it, the verse, bare though it is, has a certain limpid grandeur. But can versified theology always generate enough emotion? There are far too many passages, like the following one, which are mere bundles of dead terminology:

> I then affirm that this unfailing guide
> In Pope and general councils must reside;
> Both lawful, both combined, what one decrees
> By numerous votes, the other ratifies:
> On this undoubted sense the church relies.
> 'Tis true, some doctors in a scantier space,
> I mean in each apart, contract the place.

II, 80–6

And so on and so on. It's tedious stuff, without a glimmer of poetry, and one longs for the striking aphorism or the witty simile which Dryden once could provide.

In fact the most poignant passages in the whole poem are those in which Dryden, for once, speaks about himself. Normally he is rarely biographical and one wishes he had revealed his personal feelings more often, as he does here:

> My thoughtless youth was winged with vain desires,
> My manhood, long misled by wandering fires,
> Followed false lights; and when their glimpse was gone,
> My pride struck out new sparkles of her own.
> Such was I, such by nature still I am,
> Be thine the glory, and be mine the shame.
> Good life be now my task: my doubts are done . . .
> Rest then, my soul, from endless anguish freed;
> Nor sciences thy guide, nor sense thy creed.
> Faith is the best ensurer of thy bliss;
> The bank above must fail before the venture miss.

I, 72 . . . 149

Dryden was never one to expose his religious feelings to the public gaze, and for this reason some critics have concluded that his heart was not involved, only his intellect. Certainly his religious poems take the form of reasoned argument, and appeal to logic and common sense. But this is no proof that Dryden himself was not emotionally torn by the 'endless anguish' he speaks of, and there is another passage in this poem which gives us a moving glimpse of a troubled soul:

> If joys hereafter must be purchased here
> With loss of all that mortals hold so dear,
> Then welcome infamy and public shame,
> And, last, a long farewell to worldly fame.
> 'Tis said with ease, but oh, how hardly tried
> By haughty souls to human honour tied!
> O sharp convulsive pangs of agonising pride!
> Down then thou rebel, never more to rise,
> And what thou didst, and dost so dearly prize,
> That fame, that darling fame, make that thy sacrifice.
> 'Tis nothing thou hast given, then add thy tears
> For a long race of unrepenting years.
> 'Tis nothing yet; yet all thou hast to give,
> Then add those may-be years thou hast to live.
> Yet nothing still: then poor, and naked come,
> Thy father will receive his unthrift home,
> And thy blessed Saviour's blood discharge the mighty sum.
>
> III, 281–97

Strangely enough such confessional passages, with their beat of personal emotion, are more persuasive than the ingenious marshalling of argument or the smarting lash of satire.

Bibliography

TEXTS

Stanley Gardner (ed.): *Selections from Dryden* (Blackwell: Oxford, 1965). A good introduction and a representative selection.

Douglas Grant (ed.): *Dryden: Poems and Prose* (Penguin, 1955).

James Kinsley (ed.): *The Poems of John Dryden* (Clarendon Press: Oxford, 4 vols., 1958).

James Kinsley (ed.): *Dryden: Selected Poems* (Oxford Univ. Press, 1963).

BIOGRAPHY

Charles E. Ward: *The Life of John Dryden* (Univ. of N. Carolina, 1961).

BACKGROUND

Maurice Ashley: *England in the Seventeenth Century* (Penguin, 1964).

Christopher Hill: *The Century of Revolution, 1603–1714* (Nelson, 1961).

G. M. Trevelyan: *Illustrated English Social History*, Vol. 2 (Penguin, 1964).

CRITICISM

Louis I. Bredvold: *The Intellectual Milieu of John Dryden* (Univ. of Michigan, 1956). Chapter III for Hobbes and Science; Chapter V for Toryism.

Bonamy Dobrée: *John Dryden* (Longmans, Green, 1956).

Boris Ford (ed.): *From Dryden to Johnson* (Penguin, 1957). Includes essays on social, literary and scientific background.

147

W. Graham: *Absalom and Achitophel* (Blackwell: Oxford, 1964). A detailed analysis of the poem and background.

Gilbert Highet: *The Classical Tradition* (Clarendon Press: Oxford, 1949). See Chapter 17 on Satire.

A. D. Hope: '*Anne Killigrew* or the Art of Modulating', in *Southern Review*, I, 1963, pp. 4–14. A detailed study of the poem.

Ian Jack: *Augustan Satire* (Clarendon Press: Oxford, 1952). Chapter III, *Mac Flecknoe*, Chapter IV, *Absalom and Achitophel*.

Alan Roper: *Dryden's Poetic Kingdoms* (Routledge and Kegan Paul, 1965). Detailed study of ten poems and Dryden's royalism.

B. N. Schilling (ed.): *Dryden: A Collection of Critical Essays* (Prentice-Hall, 1963).

H. T. Swedenberg (ed.): *Essential Articles for the Study of John Dryden* (Archon Books, 1966).

Mark van Doren: *John Dryden: A Study of his Poetry* (Indiana Univ., 1960).

FOR FURTHER READING

S. P. Bovie: *Satires and Epistles of Horace* (Univ. of Chicago, 1959). A modern translation.

L. Burrows and D. Bradley (eds.): *Charitable Malice* (Univ. of W. Australia, 1955). See introduction to this anthology of satirical verse.

R. P. T. Coffin and A. M. Witherspoon (eds.): *Seventeenth-Century Prose and Poetry* (Harcourt, Brace, 1957). Selections from Hobbes, diaries of Evelyn and Pepys, Bunyan, Burnet on Monmouth's Rebellion, Dryden's essays.

Dennis Davison (ed): *Andrew Marvell: Selected Poetry and Prose* (Harrap, 1952).

Patric Dickinson: *Vergil: The Aeneid* (Mentor Books, 1961). A lively modern translation.

Bonamy Dobrée: *The Poems of John Oldham* (Centaur Press, 1960).

Rolfe Humphries: *The Satires of Juvenal* (Indiana Univ., 1958). A lively modern translation.

G. deF. Lord (ed.): *Poems on Affairs of State* (Yale Univ., 1963). For satirical verse of 1660–78.

M. H. Nicolson and D. S. Rodes (eds.): *Thomas Shadwell: The Virtuoso* (Arnold, 1966). A satirical play on scientists by Dryden's rival.

Richard Peters: *Hobbes* (Penguin, 1956).

John Plamenatz (ed.): *Hobbes, Leviathan* (abridged). Chapters I–IV (Fontana Library, Collins, 1962).

Bertrand Russell: *A History of Western Philosophy* (Allen and Unwin, 1946).

Index

GENERAL

Blackmore, 28, 33
Busby, 20
Butler, 18, 31, 32, 47
Chaucer, 42
Cowley, 22, 31, 32
Crashaw, 45
Davenant, 32, 97
Denham, 45, 74
Donne, 43
Hall, John, 22, 108
Hobbes, 29, 35, 38
Horace, 110
Jonson, 18
Locke, 21, 24
Marvell, 13, 17, 26, 27, 46, 74
Milton, 11, 13, 15, 21, 22, 28, 38, 40, 45, 73, 96
Oldham, 49
Pepys, 21, 22, 24, 26, 31
Pope, 16, 21, 24, 28, 36, 50–2, 103, 109
Rochester, 47
Skelton, 107–8
Swift, 16, 24, 32, 36
Thomson, 32, 39, 98

Waller, 44
Westminster School, 20

DRYDEN'S WORKS

Absalom and Achitophel, 13, 17, 25, 52, 54–5, 116–28
Aeneid (Virgil), 25
'After the pangs . . .', 58
Alexander's Feast, 65, 67–70
All for Love, 27
Annus Mirabilis, 35, 92–105
Astraea Redux [Charles's restoration], 14
Aureng-Zebe, 30
'Beneath a myrtle shade', 60
'Calm was the even . . .', 58
Eleonora, 82–5
Epithalamium, 62
'Fair Iris I love . . .', 61
' 'Gainst keepers . . .', 62
Heroic Plays, 30
Heroic Stanzas [on Cromwell], 13, 76
Hind and the Panther, The, 18, 26, 88, 141–6
'I feed a flame . . .', 61

Juvenal (Book Six), 56, 110–11

King Arthur, 57, 62, 64–5

Lady's Song, The, 63

Lucretius (Fourth Book), 30

Mac Flecknoe, 25, 112–16

Medal, The, 128–32

Parallel of Poetry and Painting, 91

Persius (Third Satire), 19

Religio Laici, 11, 26, 27, 133–41

Sea Fight, The, 64

Secular Masque, The, 70–2

Song for St. Cecilia's Day, A, 65–7

'Sylvia the fair . . .', 59

Threnodia Augustalis [Charles's death], 76–9

To . . . Anne Killigrew, 85–90

To . . . Dr. Charleton, 33

To Love, 64

To . . . Oldham, 53, 79–82

Upon . . . Hastings, 21, 74–6

Veni Creator Spiritus, 63

'Wherever I am . . .', 61

'Whilst Alexis . . .', 58

'Why should a foolish . . .', 61

'Young I am . . .', 60